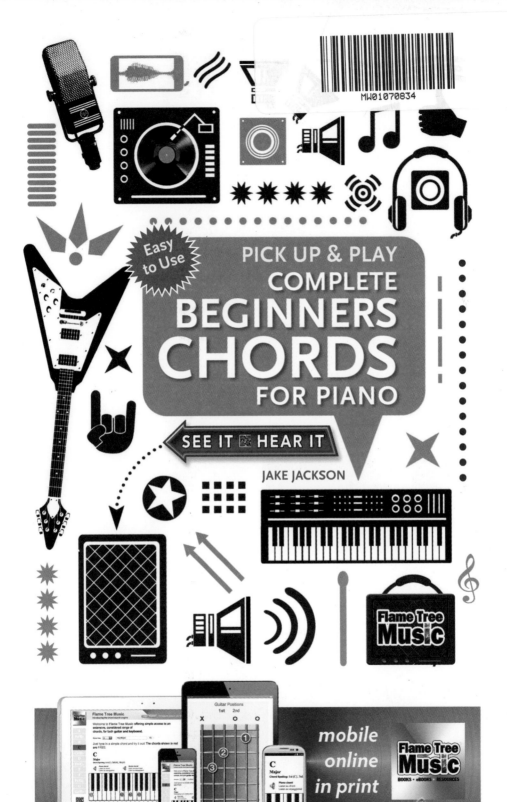

Easy to Use

PICK UP & PLAY

COMPLETE
BEGINNERS
CHORDS
FOR PIANO

SEE IT ▦ HEAR IT

JAKE JACKSON

mobile
online
in print

MW01070834

Flame Tree Music
BOOKS • eBOOKS • RESOURCES

# Contents

**Publisher/Creative Director:** Nick Wells • **Layout Design:** Jane Ashley
**Website and Software:** David Neville with Stevens Dumpala and Steve
Moulton • **Project Editor:** Gillian Whitaker

First published 2019 by
**FLAME TREE PUBLISHING**
6 Melbray Mews, Fulham,
London SW6 3NS, United Kingdom
flametreepublishing.com

Music information site: flametreemusic.com

19 20 21 22 23 24 25 • 1 2 3 4 5 6 7 8 9 10

© 2019 Flame Tree Publishing Ltd

All rights reserved. No part of this publication may be reproduced or
transmitted, in any form or by any means, without the prior permission in
writing of the publisher.

The CIP record for this book is available from the British Library.

ISBN: 978-1-78755-285-2

All images and notation courtesy of Flame Tree Publishing Ltd, except the following: guitar diagrams
© 2019 Jake Jackson/Flame Tree Publishing Ltd. Courtesy of Shutterstock.com and © the following
contributors: v74 9; BlackSnake 34; Rawpixel.com 37; Yakobchuk Viacheslav 137; ChickenStock Images
139; Dean Drobo 143; Pprapass 161; antoniodiaz 163; Dragon Images 173.

Every effort has been made
to contact copyright holders.
We apologize in advance for
any omissions and would be
pleased to insert the appropriate
acknowledgement in subsequent
editions of this publication.

Android is a trademark of Google Inc.
Logic Pro, iPhone and iPad are either
registered trademarks or trademarks
of Apple Computer Inc. in the
United States and/or other countries.
Cubase is a registered trademark
or trademark of Steinberg Media
Technologies GmbH, a wholly owned
subsidiary of Yamaha Corporation,
in the United States and/or other
countries. Nokia's product names
are either trademarks or registered
trademarks of Nokia. Nokia is a
registered trademark of Nokia
Corporation in the United States
and/or other countries. Samsung
and Galaxy S are both registered
trademarks of Samsung Electronics
America, Ltd. in the United States
and/or other countries.

Jake Jackson (author) is a writer
and musician. He has created
and contributed to over 30 practical
music books, including *Guitar
Chords* and *How to Play Guitar*. His
music is available on iTunes, Amazon
and Spotify amongst others.

Thanks to **Alan Brown** (for some of
the musical examples)

Printed in China

# Complete Beginners Chords for Piano
## An Introduction

A key component in any pianists' repertoire, chords make improvising, playing with others, and understanding music generally a lot easier. With just a few chords it is possible to learn hundreds of songs, so knowledge of the most popular chords can get you a long way. In this book you'll find:

1.  A chord section containing the most common chords: **majors**, **minors**, **sevenths** and **sus4** chords in all 12 keys.

2.  **Both left and right hand positions** for all major and minor triads, again with clear diagrams showing the keyboard and suggested fingering.

3.  A quick guide to what chords are and how they are used, covering the **different types** of chords that exist and their relation to keys, scales and other chords.

4.  A section devoted to chords in context, introducing more **advanced** chord types and examples of **simple chord progressions** to get you started with putting chords together.

5.  General advice on **playing chords** and incorporating them into your piano playing.

This book provides a good start to the basics of chords for piano: as well as clear and simple chord diagrams, there are handy reference tables and tips for jazzing up your playing technique. Plus, if you get stuck there are links throughout to our extensive audio library of chords and scales at **flametreemusic.com**.

START
HERE

THE
BASICS

A

A#/Bb

B

C

C#/Db

D

D#/Eb

E

F

F#/Gb

G

G#/Ab

CHORDS IN
CONTEXT

# The Diagrams
## A Quick Guide

**The majority of diagrams in this book are for chord shapes, though there will also be some examples of notes written in standard notation using the treble and bass clefs:**

## Standard Notation

Notes written in the treble clef generally would be played by the right hand, as its range covers notes mostly **above** middle C. Middle C is the C on the keyboard closest to the **middle** of the **keyboard**, shown here in red.

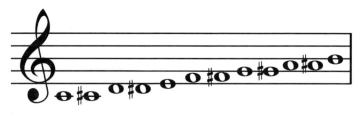

C  C#  D  D#  E  F  F#  G  G#  A  A#  B

## Bass Clef

Notes written in the bass clef are usually played by the left hand, as its range covers notes mostly **below** middle C.

C  C#  D  D#  E  F  F#  G  G#  A  A#  B

**FREE ACCESS** on iPhone & Android
etc, using any free QR code app

Scan to **HEAR** the C major chord, and
access the full library of scales and
chords on flametreemusic.com

# Finger positions

## Throughout the book the fingers are given numbers:

**For the Left Hand :**

⑤ ④ ③ ② ①

① is the thumb　　② is the index finger
③ is the middle finger　④ is the ring finger
⑤ is the little finger

**For the Right Hand:**

① ② ③ ④ ⑤

① is the thumb　　② is the index finger
③ is the middle finger　④ is the ring finger
⑤ is the little finger

**Chord Name**

**Suggested fingering**

**Starting note of the diagram**

**QR code link to the chord online**

**Right Hand**

CHORD SECTION: C

### C
Major

C♯D♭　D♯E♭　　F♯G♭　G♯A♭　A♯B♭

Middle C

① ③ ⑤

C D E F G A B

**Chord Spelling**
1st (C), 3rd (E), 5th (G)
**Right Hand**

FREE ACCESS on iPhone & Android etc, using any free QR code app

Scan to HEAR this chord, or go directly to flametreepublishing.com

65

**Names of the black notes**

**Tabs to find keys**

**Names of the white notes**

START HERE

THE BASICS

A

A♯/B♭

B

C

C♯/D♭

D

D♯/E♭

E

F

F♯/G♭

G

G♯/A♭

CHORDS IN CONTEXT

**FREE ACCESS** on iPhone & Android etc, using any free QR code app

Scan to **HEAR** the C major chord, and access the full library of scales and chords on flametreemusic.com

START
HERE

THE
BASICS

A

A#/B♭

B

C

C#/D♭

D

D#/E♭

E

F

F#/G♭

G

G#/A♭

CHORDS IN
CONTEXT

# The Sound Links
## Another Quick Guide

**Requirements**: a camera and internet-ready smartphone (e.g. **iPhone**, any **Android** phone (e.g. **Samsung Galaxy**), **Nokia Lumia**, or **camera-enabled tablet** such as the **iPad Mini**). The best result is achieved using a WIFI connection.

1. Download any **free QR code reader**. An app store search will reveal a great many of these, so obviously it's best to go with the ones with the highest ratings and don't be afraid to try a few before you settle on the one that works best for you. Tapmedia's QR Reader app is good, or ATT Scanner (used below) or QR Media. Some of the free apps have ads, which can be annoying.

2. On your smartphone, open the app and **scan** the **QR code** at the base of any particular page.

FREE ACCESS on iPhone & Android etc, using any free QR code app

Scan to HEAR the C major chord, and access the full library of scales and chords on flametreemusic.com

6

3. Scanning the chord will bring you to the C major chord, and from there you can access and hear the complete library of scales and chords on flametreemusic.com.

**FREE ACCESS** on iPhone & Android etc, using any free QR code app

Scan to **HEAR** the C major chord, and access the full library of scales and chords on flametreemusic.com

In the chord section, the QR code at the bottom of those pages will take you directly to the relevant chord on the website.

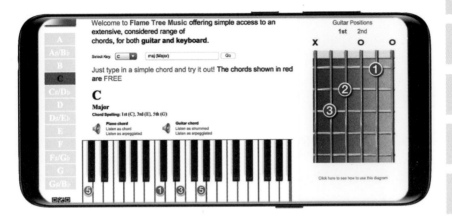

4. Use the drop down menu to choose from **20 scales** or 12 **free chords** (50 with subscription) per key.

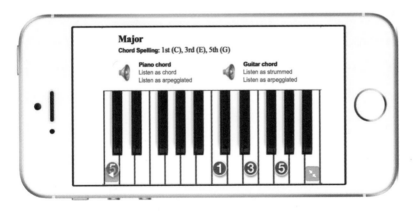

5. Click the sounds! Both piano and guitar audio is provided. This is particularly helpful when you're playing with others.

**The QR codes give you direct access to chords and scales. You can access a much wider range of chords if you register and subscribe.**

**FREE ACCESS** on iPhone & Android etc, using any free QR code app

Scan to **HEAR** the C major chord, and access the full library of scales and chords on flametreemusic.com

START
HERE

THE
BASICS

A

A#/B♭

B

C

C#/D♭

D

D#/E♭

E

F

F#/G♭

G

G#/A♭

CHORDS IN
CONTEXT

# The Basics

START
HERE

THE
BASICS

A

A#/Bb

B

C

C#/Db

D

D#/Eb

E

F

F#/Gb

G

G#/Ab

CHORDS IN
CONTEXT

**As the building blocks of music, chords play an important role in any pianist's repertoire. The sheer amount of different chords that exist can be daunting for a beginner, but this book is designed to help you identify which ones are the most useful and learn how to play them.**

Most popular songs are formed using just a few chords, as there are particular types of chords that sound better together. Understanding the relationship between chords and the notes within them is the best way to know which ones to play and when. The chord section of this book, which starts on page 40, lays out the most popular chords for each key, but to accompany that this chapter introduces the basic concepts behind chord construction.

As well as handy reference tables, this chapter includes definitions and diagrams to illustrate common terms.

**This section will cover:**

- The piano keyboard and chord symbols
- The relationship between chords, keys and scales
- Construction of chords
- Chord types within this book explained
- Common chords in each key
- Hand position and playing technique
- Different chord positions on the keyboard
- Options for tackling difficult chords

**FREE ACCESS** on iPhone & Android etc, using any free QR code app

Scan to **HEAR** the C major chord, and access the full library of scales and chords on flametreemusic.com

START
HERE

THE
BASICS

A

A#/Bb

B

C

C#/Db

D

D#/Eb

E

F

F#/Gb

G

G#/Ab

CHORDS IN
CONTEXT

**FREE ACCESS** on iPhone & Android etc, using any free QR code app

Scan to **HEAR** the C major chord, and access the full library of scales and chords on flametreemusic.com

# The Keyboard

A clear idea of where each note lies in relation to another is always useful to bear in mind. On the piano, each note is next to notes either a semitone above or a semitone below it.

**Higher** notes are on the right.
**Lower** notes are on the left.

The **black** keys on the keyboard are sharps (♯) and flats (♭). For example, in the diagram below, between C and D there is a note called either C♯ or D♭. It is referred to as either of these names dependant on the context of the other notes.

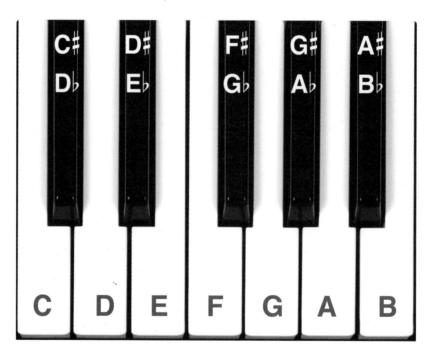

All the white notes on a keyboard exist in the simplest key in the music: **C major**. If you play all of these white notes in turn, starting from C, you will have played a **C major scale**.

**FREE ACCESS** on iPhone & Android etc, using any free QR code app

Scan to **HEAR** the C major chord, and access the full library of scales and chords on flametreemusic.com

# What Is a Chord?

START HERE

THE BASICS

A

A#/Bb

B

C

C#/Db

D

D#/Eb

E

F

F#/Gb

G

G#/Ab

CHORDS IN CONTEXT

**A chord is simply different notes sounded together. In their most basic form, chords are formed of three notes. When chords are combined they are called a chord progression.**

Below is a diagram of the C major chord. This is a great chord to start with, as it contains no sharps or flats. The C major chords uses alternate notes from the first 5 notes of the C major scale shown opposite: it consists of the root note (C), third (E) and fifth note above (G). Made of three notes in this way, it is an example of a **triad**.

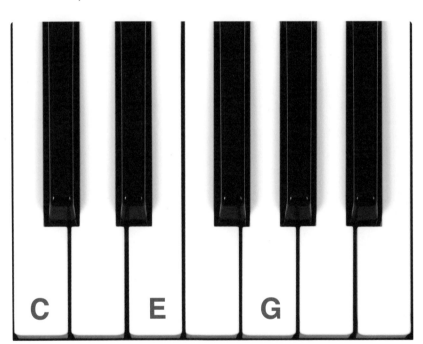

C    E    G

Altering any of these notes changes the type of chord you play. For example, if you lower (or flatten) the E by a semitone to Eb it becomes **minor**. Or, if you raise (or sharpen) the G by a semitone to G♯ it forms an **augmented** triad.

**FREE ACCESS** on iPhone & Android etc, using any free QR code app

Scan to **HEAR** the C major chord, and access the full library of scales and chords on flametreemusic.com

# Chord Symbols

START
HERE

THE
BASICS

**There are two main types of chords that form the core of most popular music: major chords and minor chords. The distinguishing feature between these relies on the 'third', or middle note of the triad.**

## Major Chords

The chord symbol that tells you when to play a major chord is simply the letter name of the chord written as a **capital**. For example, the chord symbol for the G major chord is 'G'; and the chord symbol for the D major chord is 'D'. Major chords have a **bright**, **strong** sound.

## Minor Chords

Minor chord symbols consist of the capital letter of the chord name followed by a **lowercase 'm'**. For example, the chord symbol for the E minor chord is 'Em' and chord symbol for the A minor chord is 'Am'. Minor chords have a **mellow, sombre** sound.

## Other Chords

Although there are dozens of different chord types that exist in music, all of them stem from the basic major and minor triads. Other chord types tend to just extend or vary the notes of the major or minor triads using other notes from the key.

Opposite, the most common chord types and their symbols are shown for the key of C. Not all of these chord types are present in this book, but being able to recognize the symbols will be useful, as they tell you which notes from the key are needed to form the chord.

CHORDS IN
CONTEXT

**FREE ACCESS** on iPhone & Android etc, using any free QR code app

Scan to **HEAR** the C major chord, and access the full library of scales and chords on flametreemusic.com

| Chord Name | Chord Symbol | Chord Notes |
|---|---|---|
| C major | **C** | C, E, G |
| C minor | **Cm** | C, E♭, G |
| C augmented triad | **C+** | C, E, G♯ |
| C diminished triad | **C°** | C, E♭, G♭ |
| C suspended 2nd | **Csus2** | C, D, G |
| C suspended 4th | **Csus4** | C, F, G |
| C 5th (power) chord | **C5** | C, G |
| C major 6th | **C6** | C, E, G, A |
| C minor 6th | **Cm6** | C, E♭, G, A |
| C dominant 7th | **C7** | C, E, G, B♭ |
| C major 7th | **Cmaj7** | C, E, G, B |
| C minor 7th | **Cm7** | C, E♭, G, B♭ |
| C half diminished 7th | **C°7 or Cm7♭5** | C, E♭, G♭, B♭ |
| C diminished 7th | **C°7** | C, E♭, G♭, B♭♭ |
| C minor major 7th | **Cm(maj7)** | C, E♭, G, B |
| C dominant 7th ♯5 | **C7+5** | C, E, G♯, B♭ |
| C dominant 7th ♭5 | **C7♭5** | C, E, G♭, B♭ |
| C major add 9 | **Cadd9** | C, E, G, D |
| C dominant 9th | **C9** | C, E, G, B♭, D |
| C major 9th | **Cmaj9** | C, E, G, B, D |
| C minor 9th | **Cm9** | C, E♭, G, B♭ |
| C dominant 11th | **C11** | C, E, G, B♭, D, F |
| C dominant 13th | **C13** | C, E, G, B♭, D, A |

START HERE

THE BASICS

A

A♯/B♭

B

C

C♯/D♭

D

D♯/E♭

E

F

F♯/G♭

G

G♯/A♭

CHORDS IN CONTEXT

**FREE ACCESS** on iPhone & Android etc, using any free QR code app

Scan to **HEAR** the C major chord, and access the full library of scales and chords on flametreemusic.com

# Common Keys

START
HERE

THE
BASICS

A

A#/Bb

B

C

C#/Db

D

D#/Eb

E

F

F#/Gb

G

G#/Ab

CHORDS IN
CONTEXT

The **key** of a song refers to its overall tonality, and establishes the set of **pitches** (or notes) that form the basis of the work. There are **12 keys** in western music, each with a different set of pitches associated with them. Each key also has a major or minor **mode** (or version).

There are some keys that you're more likely to come across than others. Some of the most popular major keys are:

C major

G major

D major

A major

E major

These feature strongly in most of the popular music we hear around us.

The other 7 major keys are:

B major

F major

Bb major

F# major

C# major

Ab major

Eb major

The table opposite lists the main basic major and minor chords, with page references to their chord diagrams in this book.

**FREE ACCESS** on iPhone & Android etc, using any free QR code app

Scan to **HEAR** the C major chord, and access the full library of scales and chords on flametreemusic.com

| Chord Name | Chord Symbol | Chord Notes | Diagram Pages |
|---|---|---|---|
| C major | **C** | C, E, G | *64–65* |
| C minor | **Cm** | C, E♭, G | *66–67* |
| D major | **D** | D, F♯, A | *80–81* |
| D minor | **Dm** | D, F, A | *82–83* |
| E major | **E** | E, G♯, B | *96–97* |
| E minor | **Em** | E, G, B | *98–99* |
| F major | **F** | F, A, C | *104–05* |
| F minor | **Fm** | F, A♭, C | *106–07* |
| G major | **G** | G, B, D | *120–21* |
| G minor | **Gm** | G, B♭, D | *122–23* |
| A major | **A** | A, C♯, E | *40–41* |
| A minor | **Am** | A, C, E | *42–43* |
| B major | **B** | B, D♯, F♯ | *56–57* |
| B minor | **Bm** | B, D, F♯ | *58–59* |

START HERE

THE BASICS

A

A♯/B♭

B

C

C♯/D♭

D

D♯/E♭

E

F

F♯/G♭

G

G♯/A♭

CHORDS IN CONTEXT

**FREE ACCESS** on iPhone & Android etc, using any free QR code app

Scan to **HEAR** the C major chord, and access the full library of scales and chords on flametreemusic.com

# Chord Construction

START
HERE

THE
BASICS

A

A#/Bb

B

C

C#/Db

D

D#/Eb

E

F

F#/Gb

G

G#/Ab

CHORDS IN
CONTEXT

**A key also tells you which scale can be used as the basis of the melody and which chords fit naturally into the arrangement. So, to understand a key it helps to look at its scale, which organizes all the notes of the key into pitch order.**

Different scales produce different tonalities, but they follow patterns that can be applied to each key. The patterns take the form of a set order of **tones** (whole steps) and **semitones** (half-steps). The combination of tones and semitones tells you the distance (or 'interval') between each pitch. This combination of intervals is the same in all keys for scales of the same type.

## The Major Scale

The most important scale is the **major** scale, which follows this pattern:

# T T S T T T S

When this pattern is applied to the key of C, it will produce the C major scale. Starting with C, a tone (**T**) up from C is D, then a tone up from D is E, then a semitone (**S**) from E is F, and so on. This produces the following notes:

# C D E F G A B C

On the piano, a semitone is the distance between a white note and the black note next to it, or the distance between two white notes where there is no black note in between, as in the case of E and F, and B and C. The C major scale is shown at the top of the next page in the treble and bass clefs.

**FREE ACCESS** on iPhone & Android
etc, using any free QR code app

Scan to **HEAR** the C major chord, and access the full library of scales and chords on flametreemusic.com

C D E F G A B C

The intervals between each note and the key note are called a '2nd', a '3rd', a '4th' etc. The **quality** of that interval is dependent on the number of semitones involved. For example, in major scales there are 4 semitones between the root note and the 3rd: this is called a **major third**.

## C to D = Major Second

## C to E = Major Third

## C to F = Perfect Fourth

## C to G = Perfect Fifth

## C to A = Major Sixth

## C to B = Major Seventh

If the interval distance alters, this changes its tonality and overall 'status'. For example, when 'major' intervals drop a semitone, they become 'minor'.

**FREE ACCESS** on iPhone & Android etc, using any free QR code app

Scan to **HEAR** the C major chord, and access the full library of scales and chords on flametreemusic.com

START HERE

**THE BASICS**

A

A#/Bb

B

C

C#/Db

D

D#/Eb

E

F

F#/Gb

G

G#/Ab

CHORDS IN CONTEXT

START
HERE

THE
BASICS

A

A#/B♭

B

C

C#/D♭

D

D#/E♭

E

F

F#/G♭

G

G#/A♭

CHORDS IN
CONTEXT

# Forming Triads

Chords are constructed by combining various **intervals**. Major chords, for example, are based on a **major third** interval. Using the C major scale on page 17, we can build the C major chord by taking the root note, adding the note which is a major third away from it (E), and adding the note a perfect fifth away from it (G). So, the basic notes that form a C major chord are: **C, E, G**.

It is common to number notes in a scale using **Roman numerals**, which refer to the note's position in the scale as well as the type of chord derived from it. An **uppercase numeral** means a chord built on that note is major; **lowercase** represents a minor chord.

So the scale of C major could be written as:

| C | D | E | F | G | A | B |
|---|---|---|---|---|---|---|
| I | ii | iii | IV | V | vi | vii° |
| 1st | 2nd | 3rd | 4th | 5th | 6th | 7th |
| Major | Minor | Minor | Major | Major | Minor | Diminished |

From this we can see how the 1st (C), 3rd (E) and 5th (G) notes of the major scale give the key its **major triad**, shown by an uppercase 'I'.

Using the same method to form triads for each note of this major scale would give us a **harmonized** version of the C major scale. This shows us that the following chords are all within the key of C, as they all take their notes from the scale:

**FREE ACCESS** on iPhone & Android etc, using any free QR code app

Scan to **HEAR** the C major chord, and access the full library of scales and chords on flametreemusic.com

| I: | C | (C, E, G) |
| ii: | Dm | (D, F, A) |
| iii: | Em | (E, G, B) |
| IV: | F | (F, A, C) |
| V: | G | (G, B, D) |
| vi: | A | (A, C, E) |
| vii°: | B° | (B, D, F) |

START HERE

A

A♯/B♭

B

C

C♯/D♭

D

D♯/E♭

E

F

F♯/G♭

G

G♯/A♭

CHORDS IN CONTEXT

Although triads only contain three different notes, it's easy on the piano to play more notes than this. It's common to double the root note as an **octave** note in either the right or left hand, or both (see pages 36–37). It's also possible to spread notes between the right and left hands, for example playing the full chord in the left, and just one or two in the right hand for emphasis.

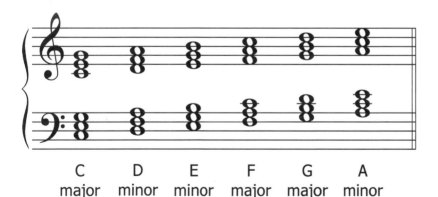

|  C  |  D  |  E  |  F  |  G  |  A  |
| major | minor | minor | major | major | minor |

**FREE ACCESS** on iPhone & Android etc, using any free QR code app

Scan to **HEAR** the C major chord, and access the full library of scales and chords on flametreemusic.com

START
HERE

THE
BASICS

A

A#/Bb

B

C

C#/Db

D

D#/Eb

E

F

F#/Gb

G

G#/Ab

CHORDS IN
CONTEXT

# Chord Types

This book focuses on the most common chord types: **major and minor triads, 7ths (major 7th, dominant 7th, minor 7th) and sus4 chords**. The tables on the following pages list the notes for these in each key and the page references for their diagrams in this book.

## Major Chords

Major chords consist of a major third interval. As seen in the previous pages, a major third is the interval from the first to the third note of the major scale e.g. in the key of C, from C to E. Major thirds are 4 semitones from the root note.

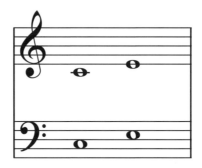

The first, third and fifth notes of the major scale make up its major triad.

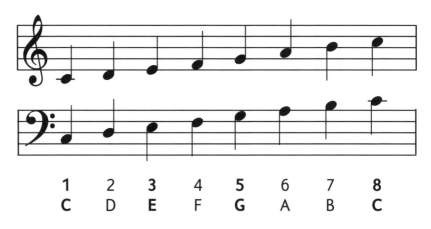

| 1 | 2 | 3 | 4 | 5 | 6 | 7 | 8 |
|---|---|---|---|---|---|---|---|
| C | D | E | F | G | A | B | C |

**FREE ACCESS** on iPhone & Android etc, using any free QR code app

Scan to **HEAR** the C major chord, and access the full library of scales and chords on flametreemusic.com

| Major Triad | Notes | Diagram Pages |
|---|---|---|
| C | C, E, G | *64–65* |
| C#/D♭ | D♭, F, A♭ | *72–73* |
| D | D, F#, A | *80–81* |
| D#/E♭ | E♭, G, B♭ | *88–89* |
| E | E, G#, B | *96–97* |
| F | F, A, C | *104–05* |
| F#/G♭ | F#, A#, C# | *112–13* |
| G | G, B, D | *120–21* |
| G#/A♭ | A♭, C, E♭ | *128–29* |
| A | A, C#, E | *40–41* |
| A#/B♭ | B♭, D, F | *48–49* |
| B | B, D#, F# | *56–57* |

START HERE

THE BASICS

A

A#/B♭

B

C

C#/D♭

D

D#/E♭

E

F

F#/G♭

G

G#/A♭

CHORDS IN CONTEXT

**FREE ACCESS** on iPhone & Android etc, using any free QR code app

Scan to **HEAR** the C major chord, and access the full library of scales and chords on flametreemusic.com

START
HERE

THE
BASICS

A

A♯/B♭

B

C

C♯/D♭

D

D♯/E♭

E

F

F♯/G♭

G

G♯/A♭

CHORDS IN
CONTEXT

# Minor Chords

Minor triads have a more **mellow, mournful sound** than major triads but, just like major triads, they also contain only three different notes.

Minor thirds are just 3 semitones from the root note. If you **lower** the major third interval by a half step it becomes a **minor third**. Just as the major third interval determines that a chord has a major tonality, the minor third interval determines that a chord is minor.

The C minor chord takes its notes from the **C natural minor scale**:

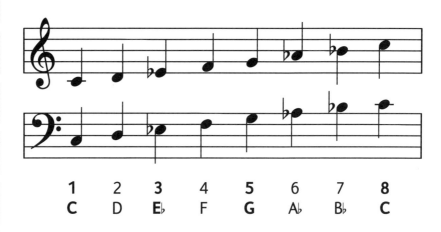

| 1 | 2 | 3 | 4 | 5 | 6 | 7 | 8 |
|---|---|---|---|---|---|---|---|
| C | D | E♭ | F | G | A♭ | B♭ | C |

**FREE ACCESS** on iPhone & Android etc, using any free QR code app

Scan to **HEAR** the C major chord, and access the full library of scales and chords on flametreemusic.com

| Major Triad | Notes | Diagram Pages |
|---|---|---|
| Cm | C, E♭, G | *66–67* |
| C#m/D♭m | C#, E, F# | *74–75* |
| Dm | D, F, A | *82–83* |
| D#m/E♭m | D#, F#, A# | *90–91* |
| Em | E, G, B | *98–99* |
| Fm | F, A♭, C | *106–07* |
| F#m/G♭m | F#, A, C# | *114–15* |
| Gm | G, B♭, D | *122–23* |
| G#m/A♭m | G#, B, D# | *130–31* |
| Am | A, C, E | *42–43* |
| A#m/B♭m | B♭, D♭, F | *50–51* |
| Bm | B, D, F# | *58–59* |

START HERE

THE BASICS

A

A#/B♭

B

C

C#/D♭

D

D#/E♭

E

F

F#/G♭

G

G#/A♭

CHORDS IN CONTEXT

**FREE ACCESS** on iPhone & Android etc, using any free QR code app

Scan to **HEAR** the C major chord, and access the full library of scales and chords on flametreemusic.com

START
HERE

THE
BASICS

A

A#/Bb

B

C

C#/Db

D

D#/Eb

E

F

F#/Gb

G

G#/Ab

CHORDS IN
CONTEXT

# 7th Chords

Major seventh chords consist of a major seventh interval. This is the interval from the first to the **seventh note** of the major scale. For example, in the key of C, this would be the interval from C to B.

There are different types of seventh chords. If you lower the major seventh interval by a half step it becomes a **minor seventh**. This interval occurs in both minor 7th and dominant 7th chords. The quality of the 3rd determines whether the chord is a minor 7th or dominant 7th: dominant 7th chords include a major third, but in minor 7th chords the 3rd is minor too.

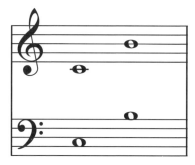

You can find the notes using the major scale, then **lower** the 3rd and 7th notes a half step if minor or dominant chords are required.

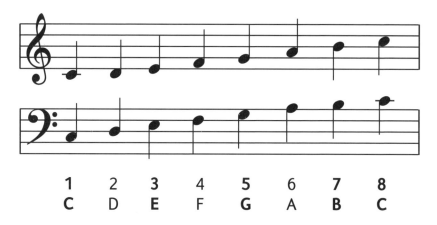

| 1 | 2 | 3 | 4 | 5 | 6 | 7 | 8 |
|---|---|---|---|---|---|---|---|
| C | D | E | F | G | A | B | C |

**FREE ACCESS** on iPhone & Android etc, using any free QR code app

Scan to **HEAR** the C major chord, and access the full library of scales and chords on flametreemusic.com

# Major 7th Chords

The major 7th chord is formed by taking the basic major chord and adding the seventh note of the major scale to it. For example, Cmaj7 contains the notes: C, E, G, B.

| Major 7th Chord | Notes | Diagram |
|---|---|---|
| Cmaj7 | C, E, G, B | *page 69* |
| C#maj7/D♭maj7 | D♭, F, A♭, C | *page 77* |
| Dmaj7 | D, F#, A, C# | *page 85* |
| D#maj7/E♭maj7 | E♭, G, B♭, D | *page 93* |
| Emaj7 | E, G#, B, D# | *page 101* |
| Fmaj7 | F, A, C, E | *page 109* |
| F#maj7/G♭maj7 | F#, A#, C#, E# | *page 117* |
| Gmaj7 | G, B, D, F# | *page 125* |
| G#maj7/A♭maj7 | A♭, C, E♭, G | *page 133* |
| Amaj7 | A, C#, E, G# | *page 45* |
| A#maj7/B♭maj7 | B♭, D, F, A | *page 53* |
| Bmaj7 | B, D#, F#, A# | *page 61* |

START HERE

THE BASICS

A

A#/B♭

B

C

C#/D♭

D

D#/E♭

E

F

F#/G♭

G

G#/A♭

CHORDS IN CONTEXT

**FREE ACCESS** on iPhone & Android etc, using any free QR code app

Scan to **HEAR** the C major chord, and access the full library of scales and chords on flametreemusic.com

START
HERE

THE
BASICS

A

A#/B♭

B

C

C#/D♭

D

D#/E♭

E

F

F#/G♭

G

G#/A♭

CHORDS IN
CONTEXT

# Dominant 7ths

The dominant 7th chord is formed by taking the basic major chord and adding the flattened seventh note of the major scale to it. For example, C7 contains the notes: C, E, G, B♭.

| Dominant 7th | Chord Notes | Diagram |
|---|---|---|
| C7 | C, E, G, B♭ | *page 70* |
| C#7/D♭7 | D♭, F, A♭, B | *page 78* |
| D7 | D, F#, A, C | *page 86* |
| D#7/E♭7 | E♭, G, B♭, D♭ | *page 94* |
| E7 | E, G#, B, D | *page 102* |
| F7 | F, A, C, E♭ | *page 110* |
| F#7/G♭7 | F#, A#, C#, E | *page 118* |
| G7 | G, B, D, F | *page 126* |
| G#7/A♭7 | A♭, C, E♭, G♭ | *page 134* |
| A7 | A, C#, E, G | *page 46* |
| A#7/B♭7 | B♭, D, F, A♭ | *page 54* |
| B7 | B, D#, F#, A | *page 62* |

**FREE ACCESS** on iPhone & Android etc, using any free QR code app

Scan to **HEAR** the C major chord, and access the full library of scales and chords on flametreemusic.com

# Minor 7ths

The minor 7th chord is formed by taking the basic minor chord and adding the flattened seventh note of the major scale to it. For example, Cm7 contains the notes: C, E♭, G, B♭.

| Minor 7th Chord | Notes | Diagram |
|---|---|---|
| Cm7 | C, E♭, G, B♭ | *page 71* |
| C♯m7/D♭m7 | D♭, E, A♭, B | *page 79* |
| Dm7 | D, F, A, C | *page 87* |
| D♯m7/E♭m7 | E♭, G♭, B♭, D♭ | *page 95* |
| Em7 | E, G, B, D | *page 103* |
| Fm7 | F, A♭, C, E♭ | *page 111* |
| F♯m7/G♭m7 | F♯, A, C♯, E | *page 119* |
| Gm7 | G, B♭, D, F | *page 127* |
| G♯m7/A♭m7 | A♭, C♭, E♭, G♭ | *page 135* |
| Am7 | A, C, E, G | *page 47* |
| A♯m7/B♭m7 | B♭, D♭, F, A♭ | *page 55* |
| Bm7 | B, D, F♯, A | *page 63* |

**FREE ACCESS** on iPhone & Android etc, using any free QR code app

Scan to **HEAR** the C major chord, and access the full library of scales and chords on flametreemusic.com

START
HERE

THE
BASICS

A

A#/Bb

B

C

C#/Db

D

D#/Eb

E

F

F#/Gb

G

G#/Ab

CHORDS IN
CONTEXT

# Sus4 Chords

Some chords are formed by **replacing** a note rather than adding one. In 'sus' chords, for example, the chord's third is replaced by the **fourth** note of the major scale in sus4 chords, and by the **second** note of the scale in sus2 chords.

Of these, the sus4 chord is more commonly used, which is why we've included a version of it in the diagrams section for each of the 12 keys.

A perfect fourth is the interval from the first to the fourth note of the major scale (e.g. in the key of C, from C to F).

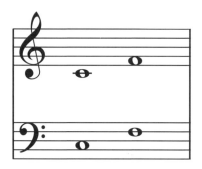

Again, you can use the major scale to find the notes:

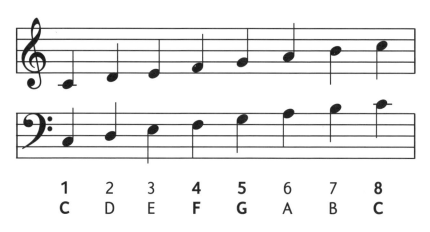

| 1 | 2 | 3 | 4 | 5 | 6 | 7 | 8 |
|---|---|---|---|---|---|---|---|
| C | D | E | F | G | A | B | C |

**FREE ACCESS** on iPhone & Android etc, using any free QR code app

Scan to **HEAR** the C major chord, and access the full library of scales and chords on flametreemusic.com

| Sus4 Chord | Notes | Diagram |
|---|---|---|
| Csus4 | C, F, G | *page 68* |
| C♯sus4/D♭sus4 | D♭, G♭, A♭ | *page 76* |
| Dsus4 | D, G, A | *page 84* |
| D♯sus4/E♭sus4 | E♭, A♭, B♭ | *page 92* |
| Esus4 | E, A, B | *page 100* |
| Fsus4 | F, B♭, C | *page 108* |
| F♯sus4/G♭sus4 | F♯, B, C♯ | *page 116* |
| Gsus4 | G, C, D | *page 124* |
| G♯sus4/A♭sus4 | A♭, D♭, E♭ | *page 132* |
| Asus4 | A, D, E | *page 44* |
| A♯sus4/B♭sus4 | B♭, E♭, F | *page 52* |
| Bsus4 | B, E, F♯ | *page 60* |

**FREE ACCESS** on iPhone & Android etc, using any free QR code app

Scan to **HEAR** the C major chord, and access the full library of scales and chords on flametreemusic.com

START HERE

THE BASICS

A

A♯/B♭

B

C

C♯/D♭

D

D♯/E♭

E

F

F♯/G♭

G

G♯/A♭

CHORDS IN CONTEXT

START
HERE

THE
BASICS

A

A#/Bb

B

C

C#/Db

D

D#/Eb

E

F

F#/Gb

G

G#/Ab

CHORDS IN
CONTEXT

# Common Chords

Some chords within a key are more important than others. For example, the key note (the '**tonic**' – C in the key of C) is usually central to establishing the **tonality** of a section of music. You can see from the example on page 19 that there are other major triads that exist within the key of C: the **I**, **IV and V** chords are all **major triads**.

C    D    E    F    G    A    B    C

I                IV    V

The V note (the '**dominant**') is important due to its strong harmonic relationship with the tonic. So in the key of C major, G occupies an important function and position in relation to C. Another tonally important degree of the scale is the IV (the '**subdominant**'). Chords built on any of these three notes help determine what key a piece of music is in.

Other useful chords in the key include the ii and vi chords, which are frequently found in chord progressions too. These most common chords are shown opposite in C, in treble and bass clefs.

**FREE ACCESS** on iPhone & Android etc, using any free QR code app

Scan to **HEAR** the C major chord, and access the full library of scales and chords on flametreemusic.com

# Common Chords of the C Major Scale

## C Major Scale

| C | D | E | F | G | A | B |
|---|---|---|---|---|---|---|
| I | ii | iii | IV | V | vi | vii° |

**I – C Major**
Notes: C, E, G

**V – G Major**
Notes: G, B, D

**IV – F Major**
Notes: F, A, C

**ii – D Minor**
Notes: D, F, A

**vi – A Minor**
Notes: A, C, E

START HERE
THE BASICS
A
A#/Bb
B
C
C#/Db
D
D#/Eb
E
F
F#/Gb
G
G#/Ab
CHORDS IN CONTEXT

**FREE ACCESS** on iPhone & Android etc, using any free QR code app

Scan to **HEAR** the C major chord, and access the full library of scales and chords on flametreemusic.com

# Relative Minors

START
HERE

THE
BASICS

A

A#/B♭

B

C

C#/D♭

D

D#/E♭

E

F

F#/G♭

G

G#/A♭

CHORDS IN
CONTEXT

**Relative** keys are keys that share exactly the same notes but have a different tonal centre (and therefore a different **tonic** note). This can be handy when moving between chords, or shifting into another key.

For example, C major and A minor are relative keys. They both contain no sharp or flat notes, but have a different tonal emphasis: A minor is a minor key, so the I, V and IV notes that would be used frequently in that key give it a different sound to I, V and IV notes used in C major. See how similar their scales are below:

**C Major**

**A Minor**

A relative minor key's note is always **three semitones below** its relative major. Or, put another way, relative minors are the **sixth degree** of the major scale (A is the sixth note of the C major scale).

The table opposite provides a quick reference of each key's relative minor, listing the minor triad notes and page references for its diagrams in this book.

**FREE ACCESS** on iPhone & Android etc, using any free QR code app

Scan to **HEAR** the C major chord, and access the full library of scales and chords on flametreemusic.com

| Major | Relative Minor | Chord Notes | Diagram Pages |
|-------|----------------|-------------|---------------|
| C | Am | A, C, E | *42–43* |
| C#/D♭ | A#m/B♭m | B♭, D♭, F | *50–51* |
| D | Bm | B, D, F# | *58–59* |
| D#/E♭ | Cm | C, E♭, G | *66–67* |
| E | C#m | C#, E, G# | *74–75* |
| F | Dm | D, F, A | *82–83* |
| F#/G♭ | D#m/E♭m | D#, F#, A# | *90–91* |
| G | Em | E, G, B | *98–99* |
| G#/A♭ | Fm | F, A♭, C | *106–07* |
| A | F#m | F#, A, C# | *114–15* |
| A#/B♭ | Gm | G, B♭, D | *122–123* |
| B | G#m | G#, B, D# | *130–31* |

START HERE

THE BASICS

A

A#/B♭

B

C

C#/D♭

D

D#/E♭

E

F

F#/G♭

G

G#/A♭

CHORDS IN CONTEXT

**FREE ACCESS** on iPhone & Android etc, using any free QR code app

Scan to **HEAR** the C major chord, and access the full library of scales and chords on flametreemusic.com

START
HERE

THE
BASICS

A

A#/B♭

B

C

C#/D♭

D

D#/E♭

E

F

F#/G♭

G

G#/A♭

CHORDS IN
CONTEXT

# Playing Techniques
## Hand Positions

**Remember, your audience wants to hear the music – not a clicking of nails on the keys.**

You will need to keep your nails reasonably short, but do not over-do it. **Play** the keys with the part of your **finger between** the **tip** and the **pad**.

Your fingers should curve gently on to the keys. Avoid straight fingers, but do not curl them up too much. Imagine your hand is a spider which needs to run along the keyboard. You can go much faster if your **fingers** are **curved** and **relaxed**.

To get the position you are aiming for, try this:

- Let a tennis ball rest in the palm of your hand, with your fingers touching it all round.

- Relax a little and remove the ball.

- Now turn your hand over; this is the position you need.

**FREE ACCESS** on iPhone & Android etc, using any free QR code app

Scan to **HEAR** the C major chord, and access the full library of scales and chords on flametreemusic.com

# Finger Numbers

We need some way of knowing which finger to use on which note. It would become very difficult to read the music if we used names such as thumb, index finger, and so on. Instead, we give each finger a number. That way, if a note should be played with the middle finger you would see a number 3 above the note on the music.

**Both hands** have their **thumb** and **fingers** numbered from **1 to 5**, starting with the thumb.

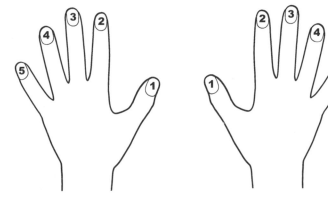

These numbers are shown in notation above or below the note. In the chord diagrams in this book, there are suggested fingerings shown in red circles for the right hand, and blue circles for the left hand.

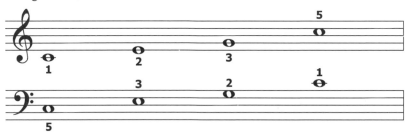

**FREE ACCESS** on iPhone & Android etc, using any free QR code app

Scan to **HEAR** the C major chord, and access the full library of scales and chords on flametreemusic.com

START HERE

THE BASICS

A

A#/Bb

B

C

C#/Db

D

D#/Eb

E

F

F#/Gb

G

G#/Ab

CHORDS IN CONTEXT

# Octaves

The previous pages have introduced you to various different intervals. Here is a reminder of the intervals in C major:

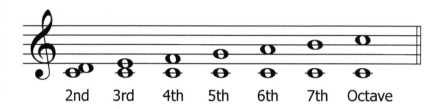

2nd  3rd  4th  5th  6th  7th  Octave

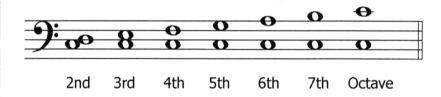

2nd  3rd  4th  5th  6th  7th  Octave

An extremely useful interval to be aware of when playing the piano is the octave. Octaves mark the point at which the 7 notes in a key's scale are repeated. When notes of the same name are played together they create a rich, enhanced sound.

**The interval between the two C notes is an octave.**

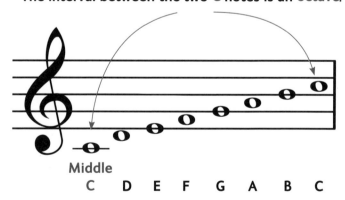

Middle
C  D  E  F  G  A  B  C

**FREE ACCESS** on iPhone & Android etc, using any free QR code app

Scan to **HEAR** the C major chord, and access the full library of scales and chords on flametreemusic.com

Often, when chords are played on the piano the root note is doubled up as an octave, either with the same named note played with the left hand, or it can also be the same named note played in the right hand too.

## C major chord

3 note chord          4 note chord

Broken chord using 3 notes

The following pages begin with a few examples of chords in use, followed by the chord section of this book, where you will find main chords for all keys, including left hand and right hand positions for all major and minor triads.

**FREE ACCESS** on iPhone & Android etc, using any free QR code app

Scan to **HEAR** the C major chord, and access the full library of scales and chords on flametreemusic.com

START HERE

THE BASICS

A

A#/Bb

B

C

C#/Db

D

D#/Eb

E

F

F#/Gb

G

G#/Ab

CHORDS IN CONTEXT

# Chord Exercises

## Chords 1

## Chords 2

START
HERE

THE
BASICS

A

A#/Bb

B

C

C#/Db

D

D#/Eb

E

F

F#/Gb

G

G#/Ab

CHORDS IN
CONTEXT

**FREE ACCESS** on iPhone & Android
etc, using any free QR code app

Scan to **HEAR** the C major chord, and
access the full library of scales and
chords on flametreemusic.com

## Chords 3

## Chords 4

START
HERE

THE
BASICS

A

A#/Bb

B

C

C#/Db

D

D#/Eb

E

F

F#/Gb

G

G#/Ab

CHORDS IN
CONTEXT

**FREE ACCESS** on iPhone & Android etc, using any free QR code app

Scan to **HEAR** the C major chord, and access the full library of scales and chords on flametreemusic.com

# A
## Major

START HERE

THE BASICS

A

A#/Bb

B

C

C#/Db

D

D#/Eb

E

F

F#/Gb

G

G#/Ab

CHORDS IN CONTEXT

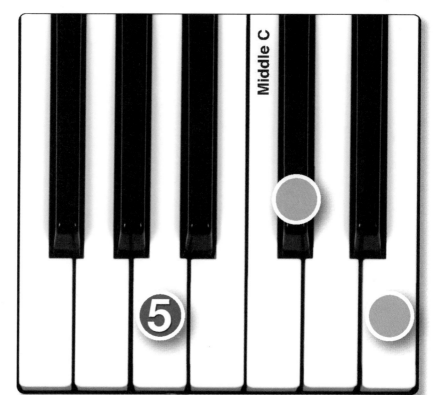

**F#Gb  G#Ab  A#Bb    C#Db   D#Eb**

Middle C

**F   G   A   B   C   D   E**

## Chord Spelling
1st (A), 3rd (C#), 5th (E)

## Left Hand

**FREE ACCESS** on iPhone & Android etc, using any free QR code app

Scan to **HEAR** this chord, or go directly to flametreepublishing.com

# A
## Major

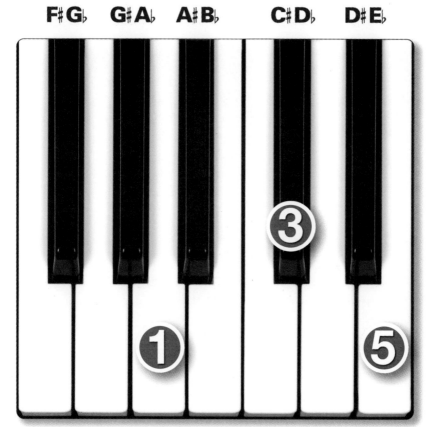

F#G♭    G#A♭    A#B♭        C#D♭    D#E♭

F    G    A    B    C    D    E

## Chord Spelling
1st (A), 3rd (C#), 5th (E)
### Right Hand

START HERE

THE BASICS

A

A#/B♭

B

C

C#/D♭

D

D#/E♭

E

F

F#/G♭

G

G#/A♭

CHORDS IN CONTEXT

**FREE ACCESS** on iPhone & Android etc, using any free QR code app

Scan to **HEAR** this chord, or go directly to flametreepublishing.com

41

# Am
## Minor

START
HERE

THE
BASICS

A

A#/B♭

B

C

C#/D♭

D

D#/E♭

E

F

F#/G♭

G

G#/A♭

CHORDS IN
CONTEXT

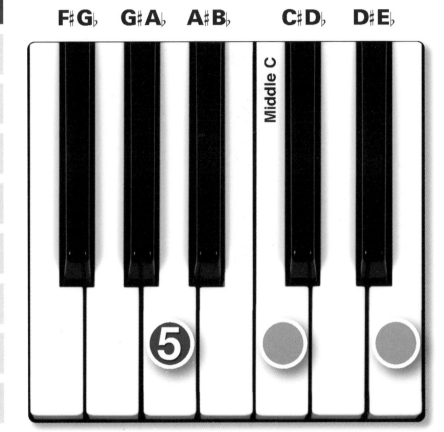

F#G♭    G#A♭    A#B♭         C#D♭    D#E♭

Middle C

⑤

F   G   A   B   C   D   E

### Chord Spelling
1st (A), ♭3rd (C), 5th (E)

### Left Hand

**FREE ACCESS** on iPhone & Android
etc, using any free QR code app

Scan to **HEAR** this chord, or go directly
to flametreepublishing.com

# Am
## Minor

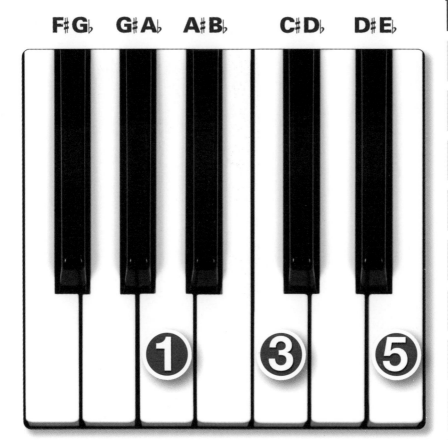

**Chord Spelling**
1st (A), ♭3rd (C), 5th (E)
## Right Hand

START HERE

THE BASICS

A

A♯/B♭

B

C

C♯/D♭

D

D♯/E♭

E

F

F♯/G♭

G

G♯/A♭

CHORDS IN CONTEXT

**FREE ACCESS** on iPhone & Android etc, using any free QR code app

Scan to **HEAR** this chord, or go directly to flametreepublishing.com

# Asus4
## Suspended 4th

START HERE

THE BASICS

A

A#/Bb

B

C

C#/Db

D

D#/Eb

E

F

F#/Gb

G

G#/Ab

CHORDS IN CONTEXT

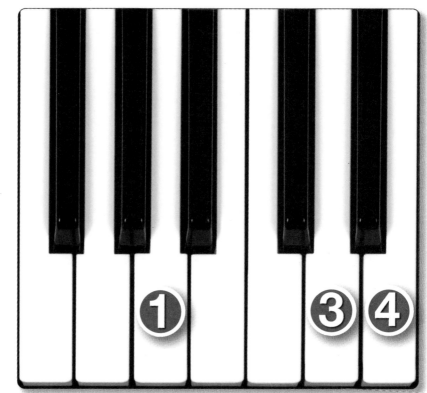

F#Gb　G#Ab　A#Bb　　C#Db　D#Eb

F　G　A　B　C　D　E

### Chord Spelling
1st (A), 4th (D), 5th (E)

**FREE ACCESS** on iPhone & Android etc, using any free QR code app

Scan to **HEAR** this chord, or go directly to flametreepublishing.com

# Amaj7
## Major 7th

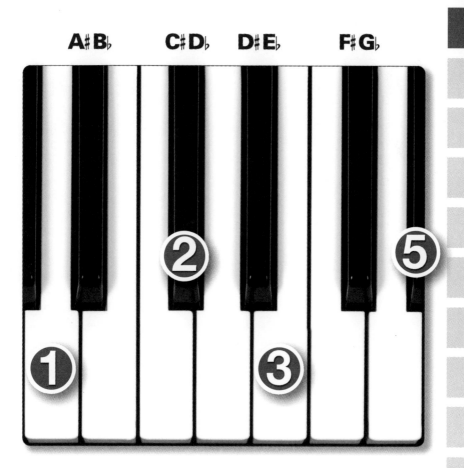

**Chord Spelling**
1st (A), 3rd (C#), 5th (E), 7th (G#)

START HERE

THE BASICS

A

A#/B♭

B

C

C#/D♭

D

D#/E♭

E

F

F#/G♭

G

G#/A♭

CHORDS IN CONTEXT

**FREE ACCESS** on iPhone & Android etc, using any free QR code app

Scan to **HEAR** this chord, or go directly to flametreepublishing.com

# A7
## Dominant 7th

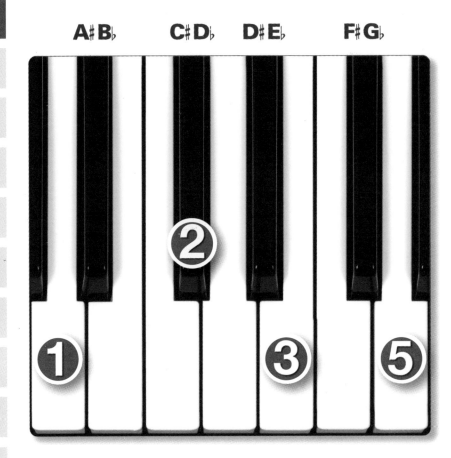

**Chord Spelling**
1st (A), 3rd (C♯), 5th (E), ♭7th (G)

START
HERE

THE
BASICS

A

A♯/B♭

B

C

C♯/D♭

D

D♯/E♭

E

F

F♯/G♭

G

G♯/A♭

CHORDS IN
CONTEXT

**FREE ACCESS** on iPhone & Android
etc, using any free QR code app

Scan to **HEAR** this chord, or go directly
to flametreepublishing.com

# Am7
## Minor 7th

START HERE

THE BASICS

A

A#/B♭

B

C

C#/D♭

D

D#/E♭

E

F

F#/G♭

G

G#/A♭

CHORDS IN CONTEXT

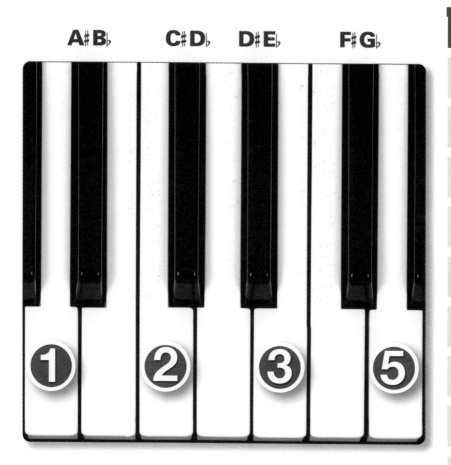

A#B♭  C#D♭  D#E♭  F#G♭

① ② ③ ⑤

A B C D E F G

### Chord Spelling
1st (A), ♭3rd (C), 5th (E), ♭7th (G)

# A♯/B♭
## Major

START
HERE

THE
BASICS

A

A♯/B♭

B

C

C♯/D♭

D

D♯/E♭

E

F

F♯/G♭

G

G♯/A♭

CHORDS IN
CONTEXT

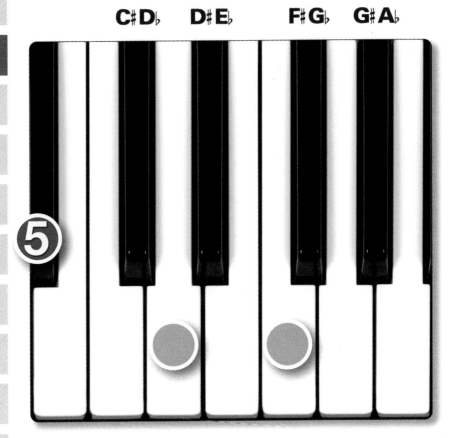

**Chord Spelling**

1st (B♭), 3rd (D), 5th (F)

**Left Hand**

**FREE ACCESS** on iPhone & Android
etc, using any free QR code app

Scan to **HEAR** this chord, or go directly
to flametreepublishing.com

# A♯/B♭
## Major

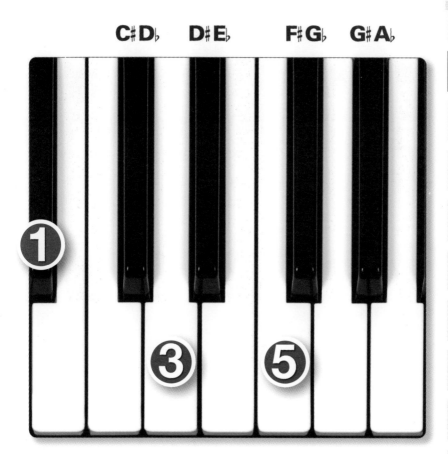

C♯D♭   D♯E♭   F♯G♭   G♯A♭

B  C  D  E  F  G  A

### Chord Spelling
1st (B♭), 3rd (D), 5th (F)

## Right Hand

**FREE ACCESS** on iPhone & Android etc, using any free QR code app

Scan to **HEAR** this chord, or go directly to flametreepublishing.com

START HERE

THE BASICS

A

A♯/B♭

B

C

C♯/D♭

D

D♯/E♭

E

F

F♯/G♭

G

G♯/A♭

CHORDS IN CONTEXT

# A♯/B♭m
## Minor

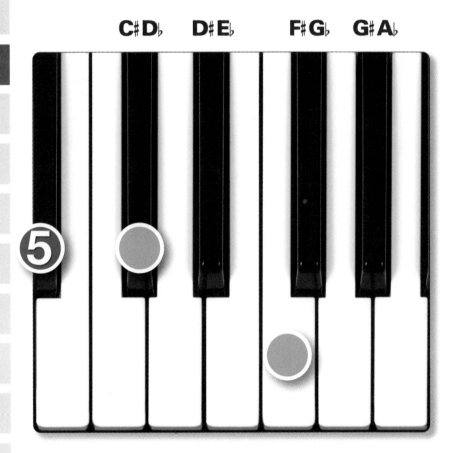

**Chord Spelling**
1st (B♭), ♭3rd (D♭), 5th (F)

## Left Hand

**FREE ACCESS** on iPhone & Android etc, using any free QR code app

Scan to **HEAR** this chord, or go directly to flametreepublishing.com

# A♯/B♭m
## Minor

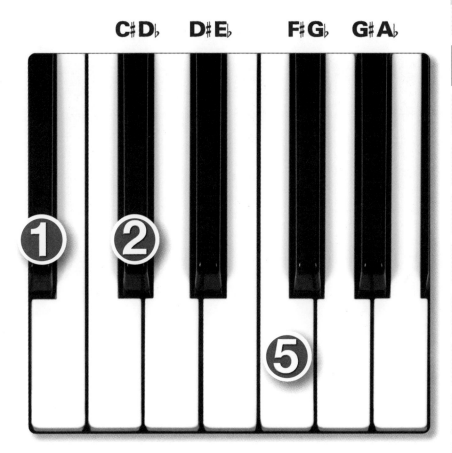

C♯D♭    D♯E♭    F♯G♭    G♯A♭

B  C  D  E  F  G  A

### Chord Spelling
1st (B♭), ♭3rd (D♭), 5th (F)

### Right Hand

START HERE

THE BASICS

A

A♯/B♭

B

C

C♯/D♭

D

D♯/E♭

E

F

F♯/G♭

G

G♯/A♭

CHORDS IN CONTEXT

**FREE ACCESS** on iPhone & Android etc, using any free QR code app

Scan to **HEAR** this chord, or go directly to flametreepublishing.com

# A♯/B♭sus4
## Suspended 4th

START
HERE

THE
BASICS

A

A♯/B♭

B

C

C♯/D♭

D

D♯/E♭

E

F

F♯/G♭

G

G♯/A♭

CHORDS IN
CONTEXT

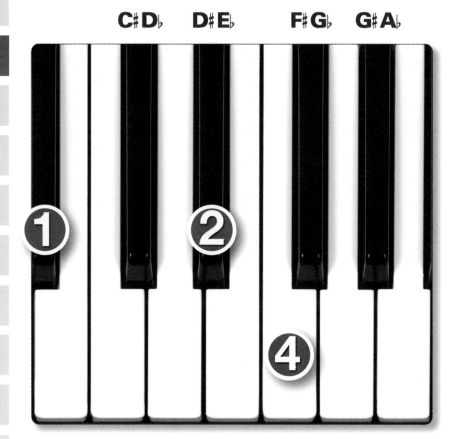

**Chord Spelling**
1st (B♭), 4th (E♭), 5th (F)

**FREE ACCESS** on iPhone & Android
etc, using any free QR code app

Scan to **HEAR** this chord, or go directly
to flametreepublishing.com

# A♯/B♭maj7
## Major 7th

START HERE

THE BASICS

A

A♯/B♭

B

C

C♯/D♭

D

D♯/E♭

E

F

F♯/G♭

G

G♯/A♭

CHORDS IN CONTEXT

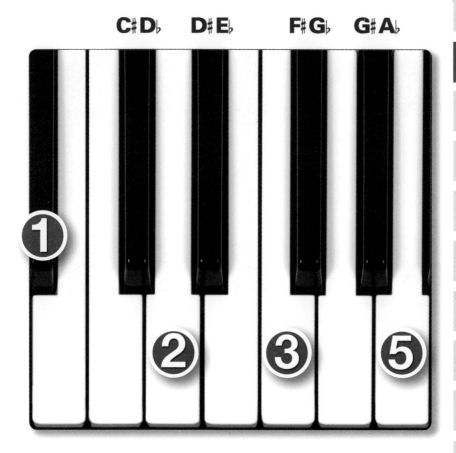

### Chord Spelling
1st (B♭), 3rd (D), 5th (F), 7th (A)

**FREE ACCESS** on iPhone & Android etc, using any free QR code app

Scan to **HEAR** this chord, or go directly to flametreepublishing.com

# A♯/B♭7
## Dominant 7th

START
HERE

THE
BASICS

A

A♯/B♭

B

C

C♯/D♭

D

D♯/E♭

E

F

F♯/G♭

G

G♯/A♭

CHORDS IN
CONTEXT

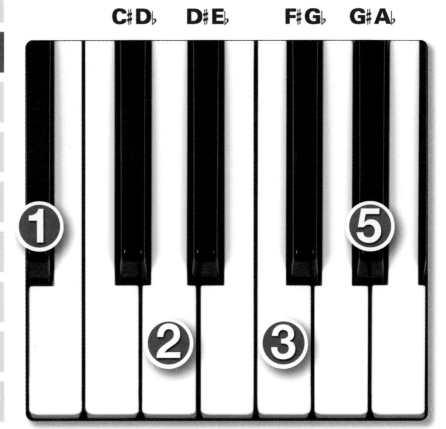

C♯D♭   D♯E♭   F♯G♭   G♯A♭

B   C   D   E   F   G   A

### Chord Spelling
1st (B♭), 3rd (D), 5th (F), ♭7th (A♭)

**FREE ACCESS** on iPhone & Android
etc, using any free QR code app

Scan to **HEAR** this chord, or go directly
to flametreepublishing.com

# A♯/B♭m7
## Minor 7th

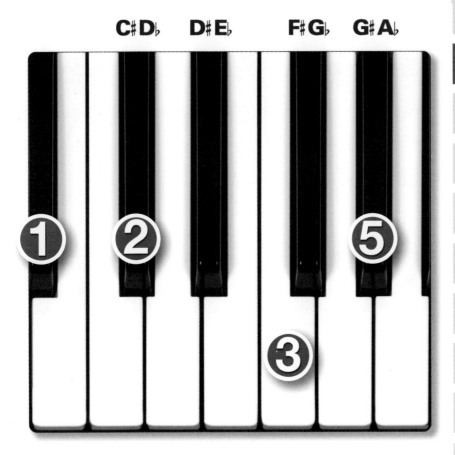

C♯D♭    D♯E♭        F♯G♭    G♭A♭

B  C  D  E  F  G  A

### Chord Spelling
1st (B♭), ♭3rd (D♭), 5th (F), ♭7th (A♭)

**FREE ACCESS** on iPhone & Android etc, using any free QR code app

Scan to **HEAR** this chord, or go directly to flametreepublishing.com

START HERE

THE BASICS

A

A♯/B♭

B

C

C♯/D♭

D

D♯/E♭

E

F

F♯/G♭

G

G♯/A♭

CHORDS IN CONTEXT

# B
## Major

START HERE

THE BASICS

A

A#/Bb

B

C

C#/Db

D

D#/Eb

E

F

F#/Gb

G

G#/Ab

CHORDS IN CONTEXT

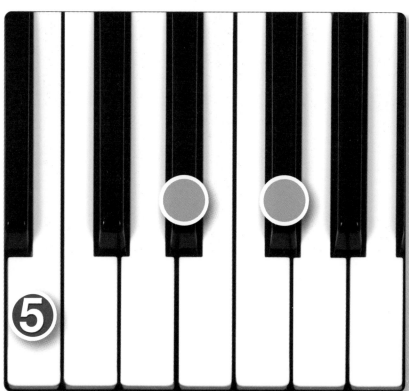

C#Db    D#Eb    F#Gb    G#Ab

B   C   D   E   F   G   A

### Chord Spelling
1st (B), 3rd (D♯), 5th (F♯)

## Left Hand

**FREE ACCESS** on iPhone & Android etc, using any free QR code app

Scan to **HEAR** this chord, or go directly to flametreepublishing.com

# B
## Major

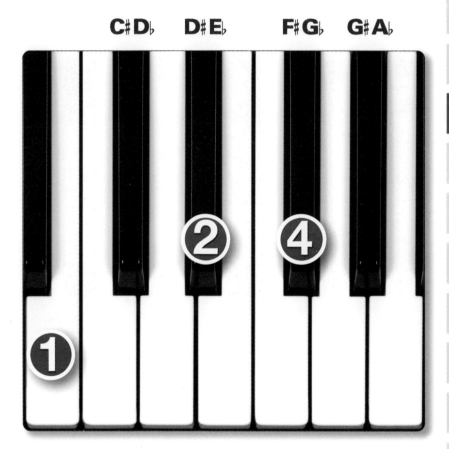

C#D♭  D#E♭  F#G♭  G#A♭

B  C  D  E  F  G  A

### Chord Spelling
1st (B), 3rd (D#), 5th (F#)
### Right Hand

START HERE

THE BASICS

A

A#/B♭

B

C

C#/D♭

D

D#/E♭

E

F

F#/G♭

G

G#/A♭

CHORDS IN CONTEXT

**FREE ACCESS** on iPhone & Android etc, using any free QR code app

Scan to **HEAR** this chord, or go directly to flametreepublishing.com

# Bm
## Minor

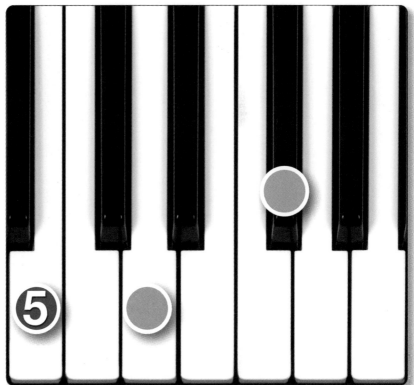

## Chord Spelling
1st (B), ♭3rd (D), 5th (F♯)
## Left Hand

**FREE ACCESS** on iPhone & Android
etc, using any free QR code app

Scan to **HEAR** this chord, or go directly
to flametreepublishing.com

# Bm
## Minor

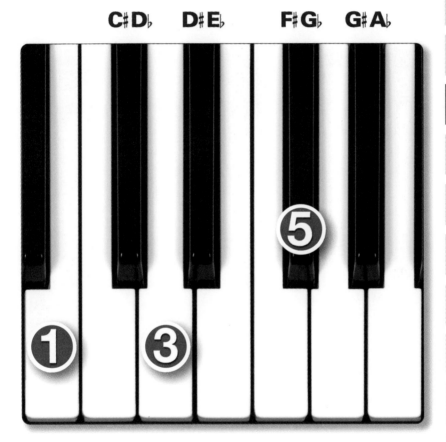

C#D♭    D#E♭      F#G♭    G#A♭

B    C    D    E    F    G    A

### Chord Spelling
1st (B), ♭3rd (D), 5th (F#)
## Right Hand

**FREE ACCESS** on iPhone & Android etc, using any free QR code app

Scan to **HEAR** this chord, or go directly to flametreepublishing.com

START HERE

THE BASICS

A

A#/B♭

B

C

C#/D♭

D

D#/E♭

E

F

F#/G♭

G

G#/A♭

CHORDS IN CONTEXT

# Bsus4
## Suspended 4th

START
HERE

THE
BASICS

A

A#/Bb

B

C

C#/Db

D

D#/Eb

E

F

F#/Gb

G

G#/Ab

CHORDS IN
CONTEXT

**C#Db  D#Eb    F#Gb  G#Ab**

**B   C   D   E   F   G   A**

### Chord Spelling
1st (B), 4th (E), 5th (F#)

**FREE ACCESS** on iPhone & Android
etc, using any free QR code app

Scan to **HEAR** this chord, or go directly
to flametreepublishing.com

# Bmaj7
## Major 7th

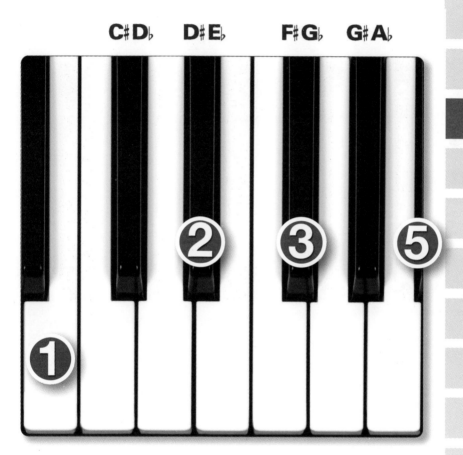

**Chord Spelling**
1st (B), 3rd (D#), 5th (F#), 7th (A#)

START HERE

THE BASICS

A

A#/B♭

B

C

C#/D♭

D

D#/E♭

E

F

F#/G♭

G

G#/A♭

CHORDS IN CONTEXT

# B7
## Dominant 7th

START
HERE

THE
BASICS

A

A#/Bb

B

C

C#/Db

D

D#/Eb

E

F

F#/Gb

G

G#/Ab

CHORDS IN
CONTEXT

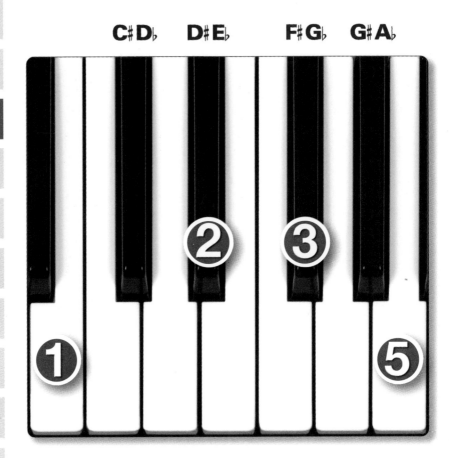

C#Db   D#Eb     F#Gb   G#Ab

② ③

① ⑤

B   C   D   E   F   G   A

### Chord Spelling
1st (B), 3rd (D#), 5th (F#), b7th (A)

**FREE ACCESS** on iPhone & Android
etc, using any free QR code app

Scan to **HEAR** this chord, or go directly
to flametreepublishing.com

# Bm7
## Minor 7th

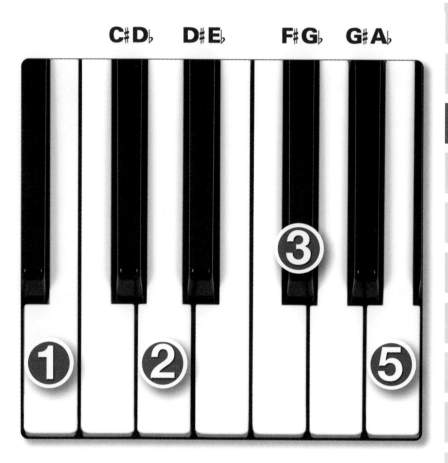

C#D♭    D#E♭      F#G♭    G#A♭

B  C  D  E  F  G  A

### Chord Spelling
1st (B), ♭3rd (D), 5th (F#), ♭7th (A)

START HERE

THE BASICS

A

A#/B♭

B

C

C#/D♭

D

D#/E♭

E

F

F#/G♭

G

G#/A♭

CHORDS IN CONTEXT

**FREE ACCESS** on iPhone & Android etc, using any free QR code app

Scan to **HEAR** this chord, or go directly to flametreepublishing.com

# C
## Major

START
HERE

THE
BASICS

A

A#/B♭

B

C

C#/D♭

D

D#/E♭

E

F

F#/G♭

G

G#/A♭

CHORDS IN
CONTEXT

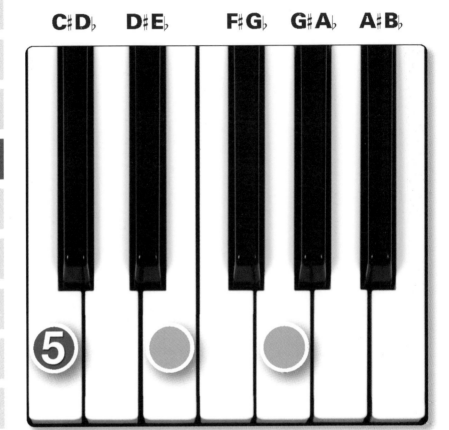

C♯D♭   D♯E♭   F♯G♭   G♯A♭   A♯B♭

C   D   E   F   G   A   B

### Chord Spelling
1st (C), 3rd (E), 5th (G)

### Left Hand

**FREE ACCESS** on iPhone & Android
etc, using any free QR code app

Scan to **HEAR** this chord, or go directly
to flametreepublishing.com

# C
## Major

START HERE

THE BASICS

A

A#/B♭

B

C

C#/D♭

D

D#/E♭

E

F

F#/G♭

G

G#/A♭

CHORDS IN CONTEXT

C#D♭   D#E♭   F#G♭   G#A♭   A#B♭

Middle C

① ③ ⑤

C   D   E   F   G   A   B

### Chord Spelling
1st (C), 3rd (E), 5th (G)

## Right Hand

**FREE ACCESS** on iPhone & Android etc, using any free QR code app

Scan to **HEAR** this chord, or go directly to flametreepublishing.com

# Cm
## Minor

START
HERE

THE
BASICS

A

A#/B♭

B

C

C#/D♭

D

D#/E♭

E

F

F#/G♭

G

G#/A♭

CHORDS IN
CONTEXT

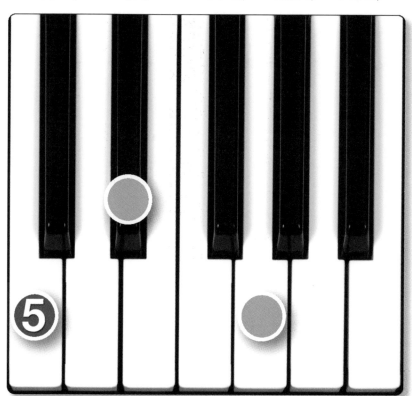

C#D♭  D#E♭     F#G♭  G#A♭  A#B♭

C  D  E  F  G  A  B

### Chord Spelling
1st (C), ♭3rd (E♭), 5th (G)

### Left Hand

**FREE ACCESS** on iPhone & Android
etc, using any free QR code app

Scan to **HEAR** this chord, or go directly
to flametreepublishing.com

# Cm
## Minor

START HERE

THE BASICS

A

A#/B♭

B

C

C#/D♭

D

D#/E♭

E

F

F#/G♭

G

G#/A♭

CHORDS IN CONTEXT

**C♯D♭**  **D♯E♭**  **F♯G♭**  **G♯A♭**  **A♯B♭**

Middle C

③ ① ⑤

**C D E F G A B**

## Chord Spelling
1st (C), ♭3rd (E♭), 5th (G)

## Right Hand

**FREE ACCESS** on iPhone & Android etc, using any free QR code app

Scan to **HEAR** this chord, or go directly to flametreepublishing.com

# Csus4
## Suspended 4th

START
HERE

THE
BASICS

A

A#/Bb

B

C

C#/Db

D

D#/Eb

E

F

F#/Gb

G

G#/Ab

CHORDS IN
CONTEXT

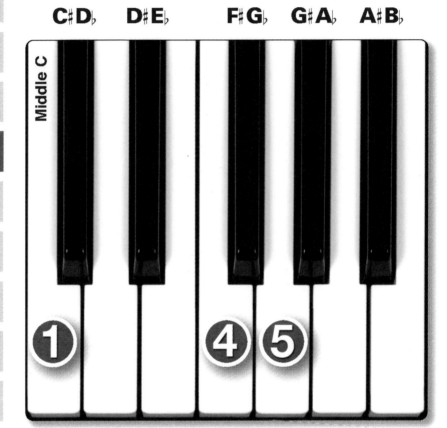

## Chord Spelling
1st (C), 4th (F), 5th (G)

**FREE ACCESS** on iPhone & Android
etc, using any free QR code app

Scan to **HEAR** this chord, or go directly
to flametreepublishing.com

# Cmaj7
## Major 7th

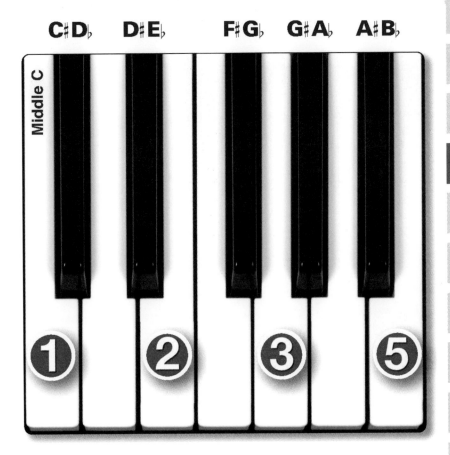

### Chord Spelling
1st (C), 3rd (E), 5th (G), 7th (B)

START HERE

THE BASICS

A

A#/Bb

B

C

C#/Db

D

D#/Eb

E

F

F#/Gb

G

G#/Ab

CHORDS IN CONTEXT

**FREE ACCESS** on iPhone & Android etc, using any free QR code app

Scan to **HEAR** this chord, or go directly to flametreepublishing.com

# C7
## Dominant 7th

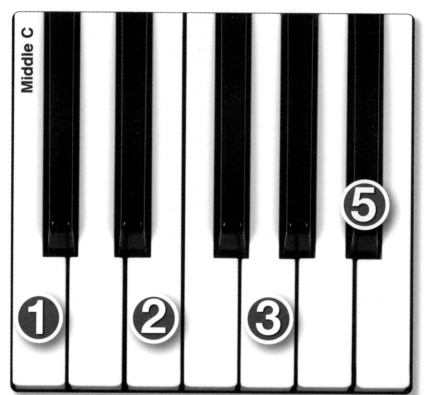

### Chord Spelling
1st (C), 3rd (E), 5th (G), ♭7th (B♭)

**START HERE**

**THE BASICS**

**A**

**A♯/B♭**

**B**

**C**

**C♯/D♭**

**D**

**D♯/E♭**

**E**

**F**

**F♯/G♭**

**G**

**G♯/A♭**

**CHORDS IN CONTEXT**

**FREE ACCESS** on iPhone & Android etc, using any free QR code app

Scan to **HEAR** this chord, or go directly to flametreepublishing.com

# Cm7
## Minor 7th

START HERE

THE BASICS

A

A#/Bb

B

C

C#/Db

D

D#/Eb

E

F

F#/Gb

G

G#/Ab

CHORDS IN CONTEXT

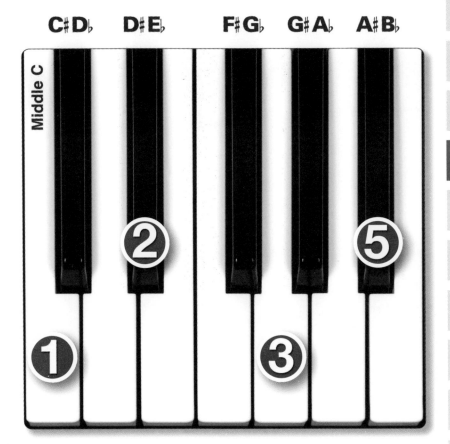

**C♯D♭**  **D♯E♭**  **F♯G♭**  **G♯A♭**  **A♯B♭**

Middle C

① ② ③ ⑤

**C  D  E  F  G  A  B**

## Chord Spelling
1st (C), ♭3rd (E♭), 5th (G), ♭7th (B♭)

**FREE ACCESS** on iPhone & Android etc, using any free QR code app

Scan to **HEAR** this chord, or go directly to flametreepublishing.com

# C#/D♭
## Major

START
HERE

THE
BASICS

A

A#/B♭

B

C

C#/D♭

D

D#/E♭

E

F

F#/G♭

G

G#/A♭

CHORDS IN
CONTEXT

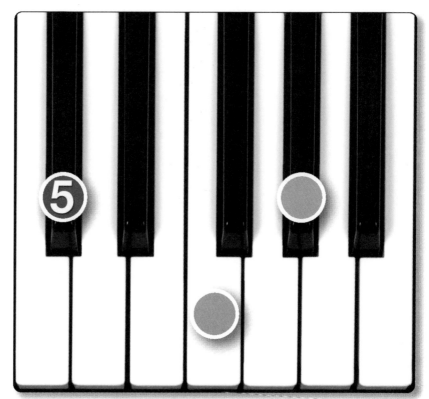

C#D♭   D#E♭        F#G♭   G#A♭   A#B♭

C   D   E   F   G   A   B

### Chord Spelling
1st (C#), 3rd (E#), 5th (G#)

## Left Hand

**FREE ACCESS** on iPhone & Android
etc, using any free QR code app

Scan to **HEAR** this chord, or go directly
to flametreepublishing.com

# C♯/D♭
## Major

C♯D♭  D♯E♭  F♯G♭  G♯A♭  A♯B♭

Middle C

C D E F G A B

### Chord Spelling
1st (C♯), 3rd (E♯), 5th (G♯)

## Right Hand

START HERE

THE BASICS

A

A♯/B♭

B

C

C♯/D♭

D

D♯/E♭

E

F

F♯/G♭

G

G♯/A♭

CHORDS IN CONTEXT

**FREE ACCESS** on iPhone & Android etc, using any free QR code app

Scan to **HEAR** this chord, or go directly to flametreepublishing.com

# C#/Dbm
## Minor

START HERE

THE BASICS

A

A#/Bb

B

C

C#/Db

D

D#/Eb

E

F

F#/Gb

G

G#/Ab

CHORDS IN CONTEXT

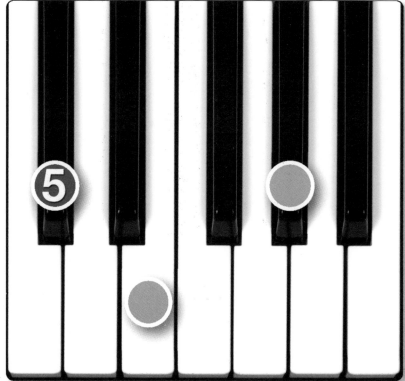

**C#Db   D#Eb   F#Gb   G#Ab   A#Bb**

**C    D    E    F    G    A    B**

## Chord Spelling
1st (C#), b3rd (E), 5th (G#)
## Left Hand

**FREE ACCESS** on iPhone & Android etc, using any free QR code app

Scan to **HEAR** this chord, or go directly to flametreepublishing.com

# C♯/D♭m
## Minor

START HERE

THE BASICS

A

A♯/B♭

B

C

C♯/D♭

D

D♯/E♭

E

F

F♯/G♭

G

G♯/A♭

CHORDS IN CONTEXT

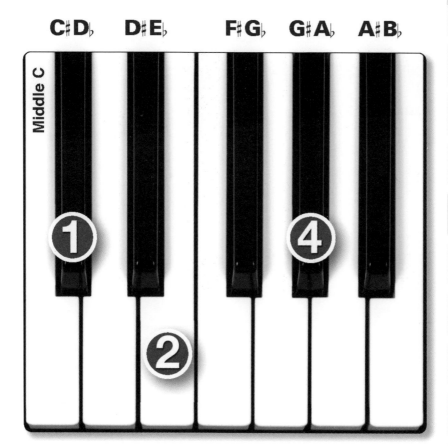

**Chord Spelling**
1st (C♯), ♭3rd (E), 5th (G♯)

## Right Hand

**FREE ACCESS** on iPhone & Android etc, using any free QR code app

Scan to **HEAR** this chord, or go directly to flametreepublishing.com

# C#/D♭sus4
## Suspended 4th

START
HERE

THE
BASICS

A

A#/B♭

B

C

C#/D♭

D

D#/E♭

E

F

F#/G♭

G

G#/A♭

CHORDS IN
CONTEXT

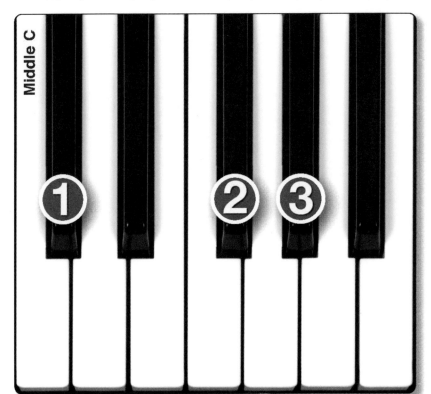

**Chord Spelling**
1st (C#), 4th (F#), 5th (G#)

**FREE ACCESS** on iPhone & Android
etc, using any free QR code app

Scan to **HEAR** this chord, or go directly
to flametreepublishing.com

# C#/D♭maj7
## Major 7th

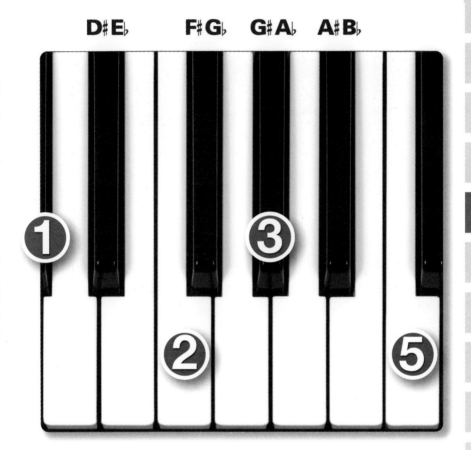

D#E♭     F#G♭   G#A♭   A#B♭

D   E   F   G   A   B   C

### Chord Spelling
1st (C#), 3rd (E#), 5th (G#), 7th (B#)

START HERE

THE BASICS

A

A#/B♭

B

C

C#/D♭

D

D#/E♭

E

F

F#/G♭

G

G#/A♭

CHORDS IN CONTEXT

**FREE ACCESS** on iPhone & Android etc, using any free QR code app

Scan to **HEAR** this chord, or go directly to flametreepublishing.com

77

# C♯/D♭7
## Dominant 7th

START
HERE

THE
BASICS

A

A♯/B♭

B

C

C♯/D♭

D

D♯/E♭

E

F

F♯/G♭

G

G♯/A♭

CHORDS IN
CONTEXT

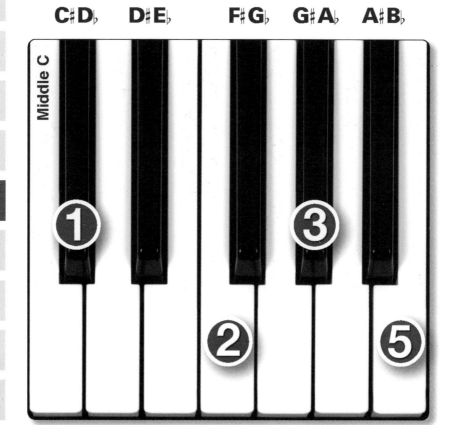

## Chord Spelling
1st (C♯), 3rd (E♯), 5th (G♯), ♭7th (B)

**FREE ACCESS** on iPhone & Android
etc, using any free QR code app

Scan to **HEAR** this chord, or go directly
to flametreepublishing.com

# C♯/D♭m7
## Minor 7th

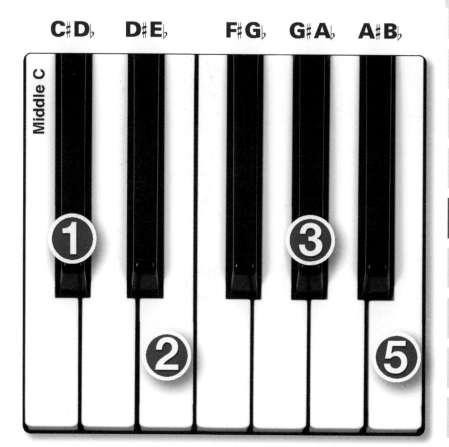

### Chord Spelling
1st (C♯), ♭3rd (E), 5th (G♯), ♭7th (B)

**FREE ACCESS** on iPhone & Android etc, using any free QR code app

Scan to **HEAR** this chord, or go directly to flametreepublishing.com

START HERE

THE BASICS

A

A♯/B♭

B

C

C♯/D♭

D

D♯/E♭

E

F

F♯/G♭

G

G♯/A♭

CHORDS IN CONTEXT

# D
## Major

START
HERE

THE
BASICS

A

A#/Bb

B

C

C#/Db

D

D#/Eb

E

F

F#/Gb

G

G#/Ab

CHORDS IN
CONTEXT

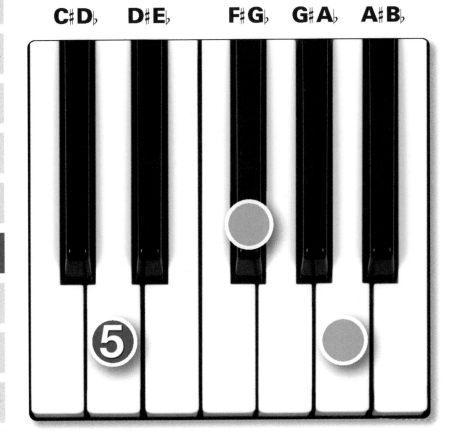

### Chord Spelling
1st (D), 3rd (F#), 5th (A)

### Left Hand

# D
## Major

START HERE

THE BASICS

A

A#/B♭

B

C

C#/D♭

D

D#/E♭

E

F

F#/G♭

G

G#/A♭

CHORDS IN CONTEXT

C#D♭   D#E♭       F#G♭   G#A♭   A#B♭

Middle C

① ② ④

C   D   E   F   G   A   B

### Chord Spelling
1st (D), 3rd (F#), 5th (A)

### Right Hand

# Dm
## Minor

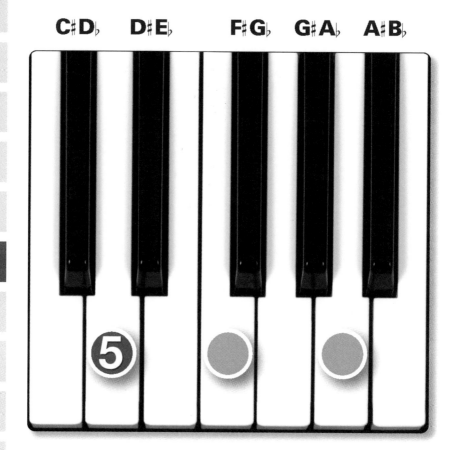

C♯D♭ D♯E♭ F♯G♭ G♯A♭ A♯B♭

C D E F G A B

### Chord Spelling
1st (D), ♭3rd (F), 5th (A)

### Left Hand

START HERE

THE BASICS

A

A♯/B♭

B

C

C♯/D♭

D

D♯/E♭

E

F

F♯/G♭

G

G♯/A♭

CHORDS IN CONTEXT

**FREE ACCESS** on iPhone & Android etc, using any free QR code app

Scan to **HEAR** this chord, or go directly to flametreepublishing.com

# Dm
## Minor

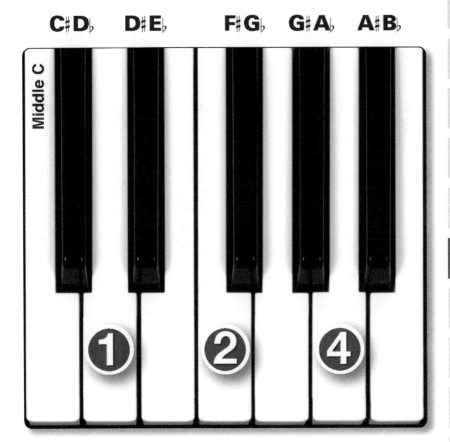

**Chord Spelling**

1st (D), ♭3rd (F), 5th (A)

## Right Hand

**FREE ACCESS** on iPhone & Android etc, using any free QR code app

Scan to **HEAR** this chord, or go directly to flametreepublishing.com

START HERE

THE BASICS

A

A♯/B♭

B

C

C♯/D♭

D

D♯/E♭

E

F

F♯/G♭

G

G♯/A♭

CHORDS IN CONTEXT

# Dsus4
## Suspended 4th

START
HERE

THE
BASICS

A

A#/B♭

B

C

C#/D♭

D

D#/E♭

E

F

F#/G♭

G

G#/A♭

CHORDS IN
CONTEXT

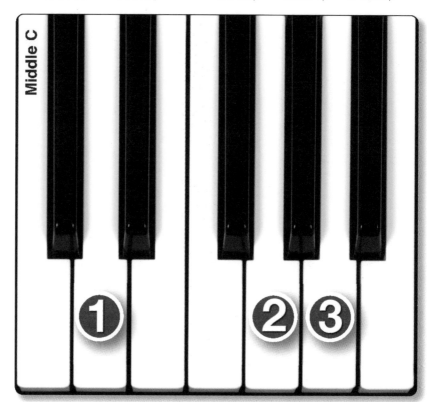

**C#D♭  D#E♭   F#G♭  G#A♭  A#B♭**

Middle C

① ② ③

**C D E F G A B**

### Chord Spelling
1st (D), 4th (G), 5th (A)

**FREE ACCESS** on iPhone & Android
etc, using any free QR code app

Scan to **HEAR** this chord, or go directly
to flametreepublishing.com

# Dmaj7
## Major 7th

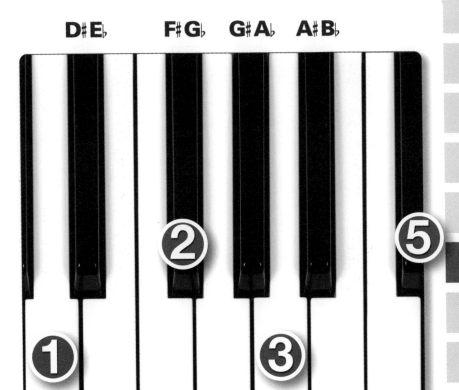

**D#E♭  F#G♭  G#A♭  A#B♭**

D E F G A B C

### Chord Spelling
1st (D), 3rd (F#), 5th (A), 7th (C#)

**FREE ACCESS** on iPhone & Android etc, using any free QR code app

Scan to **HEAR** this chord, or go directly to flametreepublishing.com

START HERE
THE BASICS
A
A#/B♭
B
C
C#/D♭
D
D#/E♭
E
F
F#/G♭
G
G#/A♭
CHORDS IN CONTEXT

85

# D7
## Dominant 7th

START
HERE

THE
BASICS

A

A#/B♭

B

C

C#/D♭

D

D#/E♭

E

F

F#/G♭

G

G#/A♭

CHORDS IN
CONTEXT

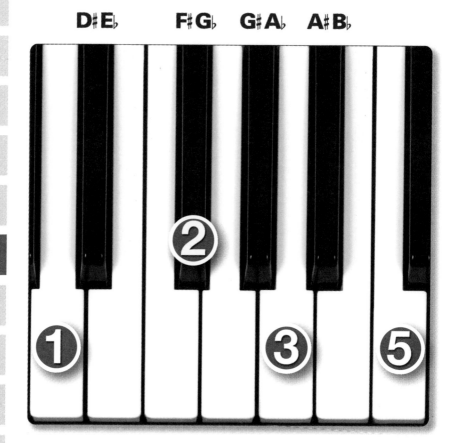

**D♯E♭**    **F♯G♭**    **G♯A♭**    **A♯B♭**

D    E    F    G    A    B    C

### Chord Spelling
1st (D), 3rd (F♯), 5th (A), ♭7th (C)

**FREE ACCESS** on iPhone & Android
etc, using any free QR code app

Scan to **HEAR** this chord, or go directly
to flametreepublishing.com

# Dm7
## Minor 7th

START HERE

THE BASICS

A

A#/B♭

B

C

C#/D♭

D

D#/E♭

E

F

F#/G♭

G

G#/A♭

CHORDS IN CONTEXT

**Chord Spelling**

1st (D), ♭3rd (F), 5th (A), ♭7th (C)

**FREE ACCESS** on iPhone & Android etc, using any free QR code app

Scan to **HEAR** this chord, or go directly to flametreepublishing.com

# D♯/E♭
## Major

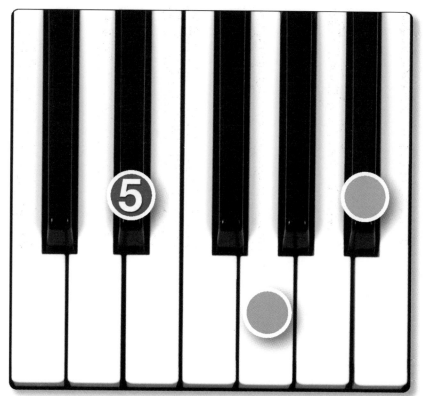

C♯D♭  D♯E♭    F♯G♭  G♯A♭  A♯B♭

C   D   E   F   G   A   B

### Chord Spelling
1st (E♭), 3rd (G), 5th (B♭)

### Left Hand

**FREE ACCESS** on iPhone & Android etc, using any free QR code app

Scan to **HEAR** this chord, or go directly to flametreepublishing.com

# D#/E♭
## Major

C#D♭    D#E♭    F#G♭   G#A♭   A#B♭

Middle C

① ④ ②

C D E F G A B

### Chord Spelling
1st (E♭), 3rd (G), 5th (B♭)

## Right Hand

**FREE ACCESS** on iPhone & Android etc, using any free QR code app

Scan to **HEAR** this chord, or go directly to flametreepublishing.com

START HERE

THE BASICS

A

A#/B♭

B

C

C#/D♭

D

D#/E♭

E

F

F#/G♭

G

G#/A♭

CHORDS IN CONTEXT

# D#/E♭m
## Minor

START HERE

THE BASICS

A

A#/B♭

B

C

C#/D♭

D

D#/E♭

E

F

F#/G♭

G

G#/A♭

CHORDS IN CONTEXT

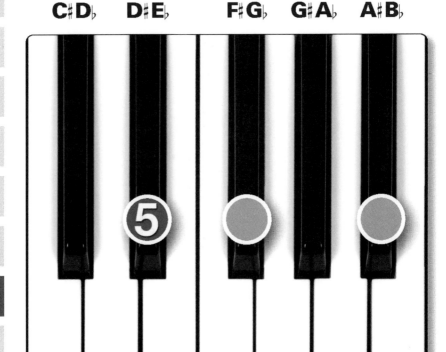

C#D♭  D#E♭  F#G♭  G#A♭  A#B♭

C D E F G A B

### Chord Spelling
1st (E♭), ♭3rd (G♭), 5th (B♭)

### Left Hand

**FREE ACCESS** on iPhone & Android etc, using any free QR code app

Scan to **HEAR** this chord, or go directly to flametreepublishing.com

# D#/E♭m
## Minor

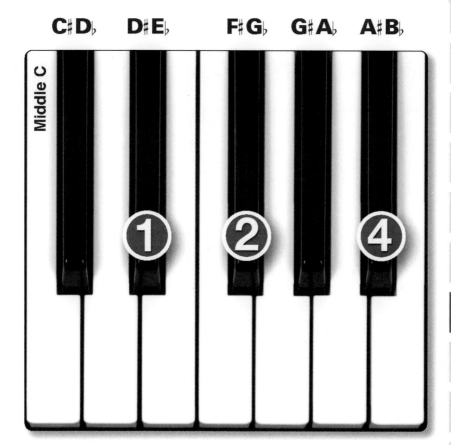

**Chord Spelling**

1st (E♭), ♭3rd (G♭), 5th (B♭)

## Right Hand

**FREE ACCESS** on iPhone & Android etc, using any free QR code app

Scan to **HEAR** this chord, or go directly to flametreepublishing.com

# D♯/E♭sus4
## Suspended 4th

START HERE

THE BASICS

A

A♯/B♭

B

C

C♯/D♭

D

D♯/E♭

E

F

F♯/G♭

G

G♯/A♭

CHORDS IN CONTEXT

### Chord Spelling
1st (E♭), 4th (A♭), 5th (B♭)

**FREE ACCESS** on iPhone & Android etc, using any free QR code app

Scan to **HEAR** this chord, or go directly to flametreepublishing.com

# D#/Ebmaj7
## Major 7th

START
HERE

THE
BASICS

A

A#/Bb

B

C

C#/Db

D

D#/Eb

E

F

F#/Gb

G

G#/Ab

CHORDS IN
CONTEXT

F#Gb   G#Ab   A#Bb      C#Db

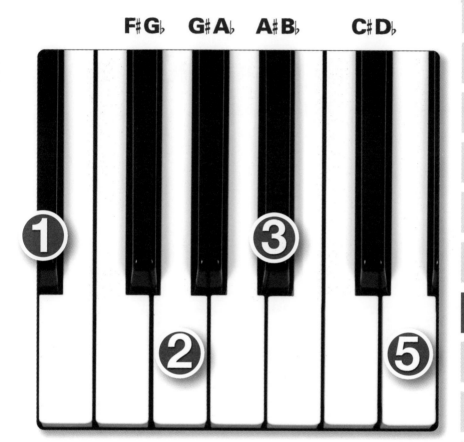

E    F    G    A    B    C    D

### Chord Spelling
1st (Eb), 3rd (G), 5th (Bb), 7th (D)

**FREE ACCESS** on iPhone & Android etc,
using any free QR code app

Scan to **HEAR** this chord, or go directly
to flametreepublishing.com

# D♯/E♭7
## Dominant 7th

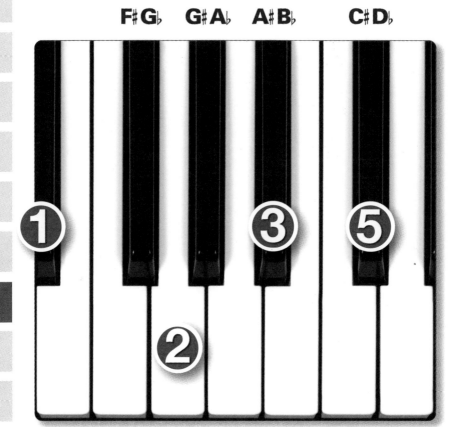

F♯G♭  G♯A♭  A♯B♭  C♯D♭

E F G A B C D

## Chord Spelling
1st (E♭), 3rd (G), 5th (B♭), ♭7th (D♭)

**FREE ACCESS** on iPhone & Android
etc, using any free QR code app

Scan to **HEAR** this chord, or go directly
to flametreepublishing.com

START HERE

THE BASICS

A

A♯/B♭

B

C

C♯/D♭

D

D♯/E♭

E

F

F♯/G♭

G

G♯/A♭

CHORDS IN CONTEXT

# D♯/E♭m7
## Minor 7th

START HERE

THE BASICS

A

A♯/B♭

B

C

C♯/D♭

D

D♯/E♭

E

F

F♯/G♭

G

G♯/A♭

CHORDS IN CONTEXT

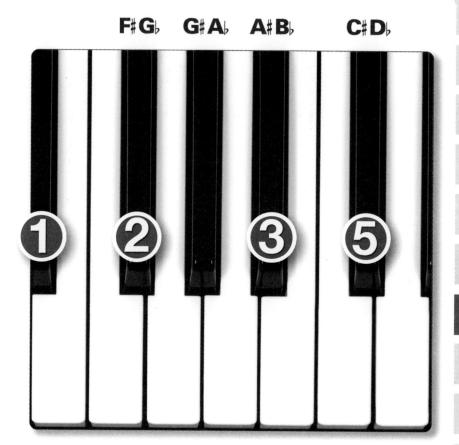

**F♯G♭   G♯A♭   A♯B♭        C♯D♭**

① ② ③ ⑤

**E    F    G    A    B    C    D**

## Chord Spelling
1st (E♭), ♭3rd (G♭), 5th (B♭), ♭7th (D♭)

**FREE ACCESS** on iPhone & Android etc, using any free QR code app

Scan to **HEAR** this chord, or go directly to flametreepublishing.com

# E
## Major

START
HERE

THE
BASICS

A

A#/B♭

B

C

C#/D♭

D

D#/E♭

E

F

F#/G♭

G

G#/A♭

CHORDS IN
CONTEXT

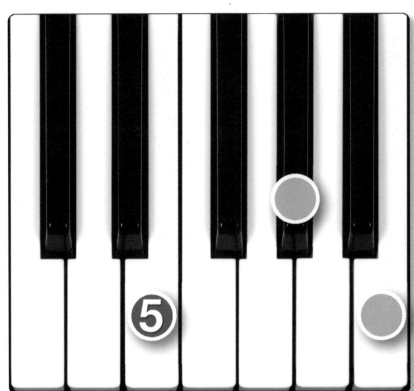

**C#D♭**  **D#E♭**  **F#G♭**  **G#A♭**  **A#B♭**

C D E F G A B

## Chord Spelling
1st (E), 3rd (G♯), 5th (B)

## Left Hand

**FREE ACCESS** on iPhone & Android
etc, using any free QR code app

Scan to **HEAR** this chord, or go directly
to flametreepublishing.com

# E
## Major

START HERE

THE BASICS

A

A#/B♭

B

C

C#/D♭

D

D#/E♭

E

F

F#/G♭

G

G#/A♭

CHORDS IN CONTEXT

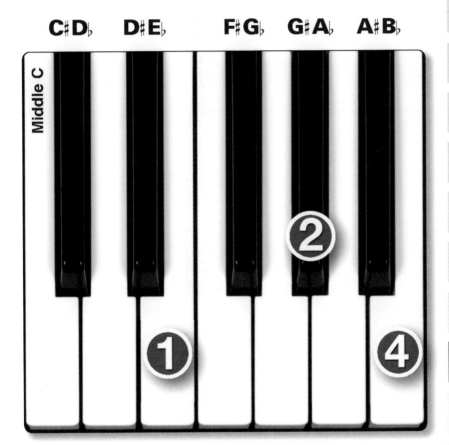

C#D♭    D#E♭    F#G♭    G#A♭    A#B♭

Middle C

C    D    E    F    G    A    B

### Chord Spelling
1st (E), 3rd (G♯), 5th (B)

### Right Hand

**FREE ACCESS** on iPhone & Android etc, using any free QR code app

Scan to **HEAR** this chord, or go directly to flametreepublishing.com

# Em
## Minor

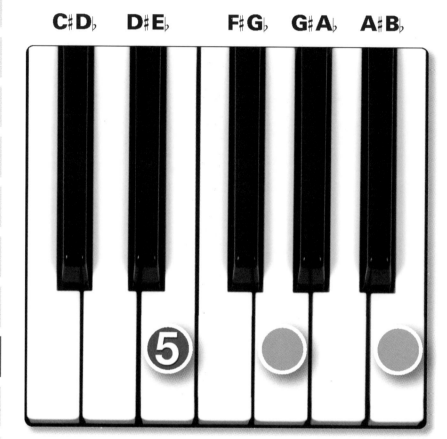

**C♯D♭**  **D♯E♭**  **F♯G♭**  **G♯A♭**  **A♯B♭**

**C  D  E  F  G  A  B**

## Chord Spelling
1st (E), ♭3rd (G), 5th (B)

## Left Hand

**FREE ACCESS** on iPhone & Android etc, using any free QR code app

Scan to **HEAR** this chord, or go directly to flametreepublishing.com

Sidebar navigation:
START HERE
THE BASICS
A
A♯/B♭
B
C
C♯/D♭
D
D♯/E♭
E
F
F♯/G♭
G
G♯/A♭
CHORDS IN CONTEXT

# Em
## Minor

C#D♭    D#E♭     F#G♭    G#A♭    A#B♭

Middle C

① ② ④

C   D   E   F   G   A   B

### Chord Spelling
1st (E), ♭3rd (G), 5th (B)

## Right Hand

START HERE

THE BASICS

A

A#/B♭

B

C

C#/D♭

D

D#/E♭

E

F

F#/G♭

G

G#/A♭

CHORDS IN CONTEXT

**FREE ACCESS** on iPhone & Android etc, using any free QR code app

Scan to **HEAR** this chord, or go directly to flametreepublishing.com

# Esus4
## Suspended 4th

START
HERE

THE
BASICS

A

A#/Bb

B

C

C#/Db

D

D#/Eb

E

F

F#/Gb

G

G#/Ab

CHORDS IN
CONTEXT

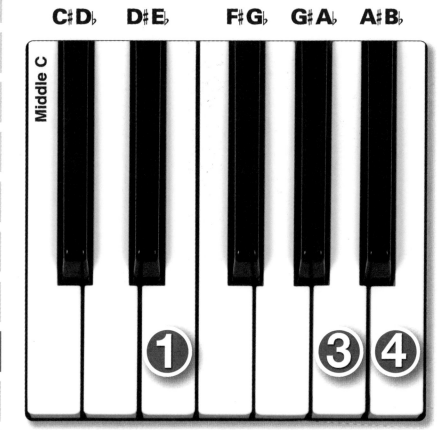

## Chord Spelling
1st (E), 4th (A), 5th (B)

**FREE ACCESS** on iPhone & Android
etc, using any free QR code app

Scan to **HEAR** this chord, or go directly
to flametreepublishing.com

# Emaj7
## Major 7th

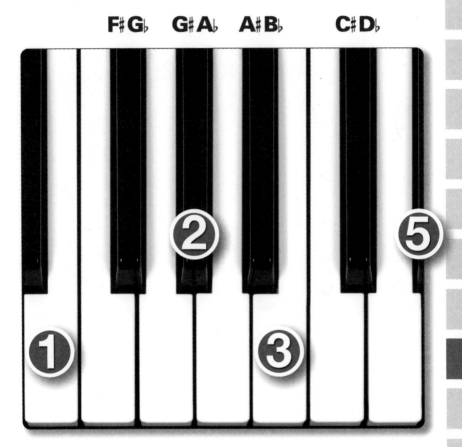

F#G♭   G#A♭   A#B♭      C#D♭

E  F  G  A  B  C  D

**START HERE**

**THE BASICS**

**A**

**A#/B♭**

**B**

**C**

**C#/D♭**

**D**

**D#/E♭**

**E**

**F**

**F#/G♭**

**G**

**G#/A♭**

**CHORDS IN CONTEXT**

### Chord Spelling
1st (E), 3rd (G♯), 5th (B), 7th (D♯)

**FREE ACCESS** on iPhone & Android etc, using any free QR code app

Scan to **HEAR** this chord, or go directly to flametreepublishing.com

# E7
## Dominant 7th

START
HERE

THE
BASICS

A

A#/Bb

B

C

C#/Db

D

D#/Eb

E

F

F#/Gb

G

G#/Ab

CHORDS IN
CONTEXT

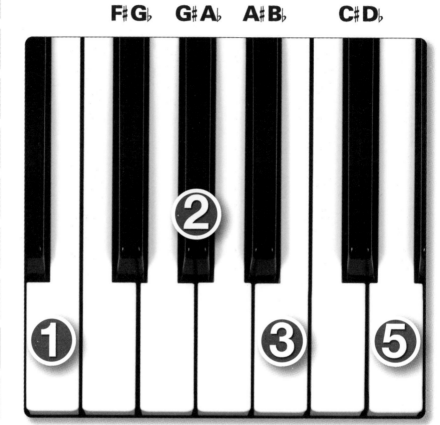

### Chord Spelling
1st (E), 3rd (G#), 5th (B), b7th (D)

**FREE ACCESS** on iPhone & Android
etc, using any free QR code app

Scan to **HEAR** this chord, or go directly
to flametreepublishing.com

# Em7
## Minor 7th

**Chord Spelling**
1st (E), ♭3rd (G), 5th (B), ♭7th (D)

START
HERE

THE
BASICS

A

A#/B♭

B

C

C#/D♭

D

D#/E♭

E

F

F#/G♭

G

G#/A♭

CHORDS IN
CONTEXT

**FREE ACCESS** on iPhone & Android etc, using any free QR code app

Scan to **HEAR** this chord, or go directly to flametreepublishing.com

# F
## Major

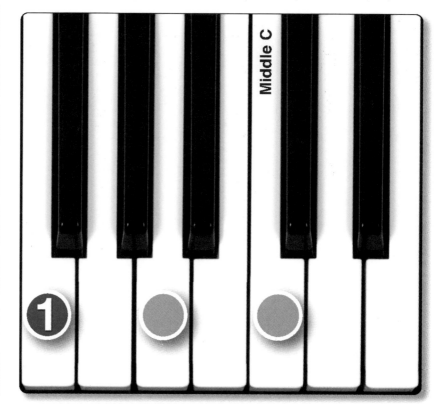

**Chord Spelling**

1st (F), 3rd (A), 5th (C)

## Left Hand

**FREE ACCESS** on iPhone & Android etc, using any free QR code app

Scan to **HEAR** this chord, or go directly to flametreepublishing.com

# F
## Major

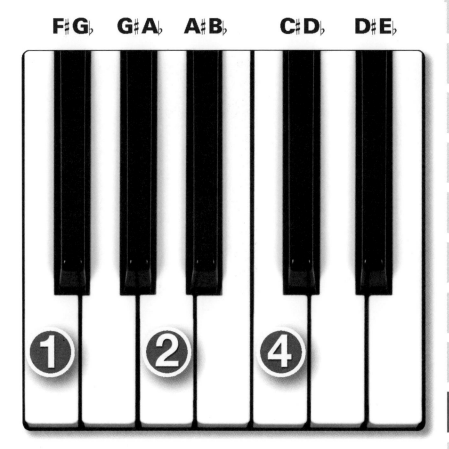

F#G♭  G#A♭  A#B♭    C#D♭   D#E♭

F   G   A   B   C   D   E

### Chord Spelling
1st (F), 3rd (A), 5th (C)

## Right Hand

**FREE ACCESS** on iPhone & Android etc, using any free QR code app

Scan to **HEAR** this chord, or go directly to flametreepublishing.com

START HERE

THE BASICS

A

A#/B♭

B

C

C#/D♭

D

D#/E♭

E

F

F#/G♭

G

G#/A♭

CHORDS IN CONTEXT

# Fm
## Minor

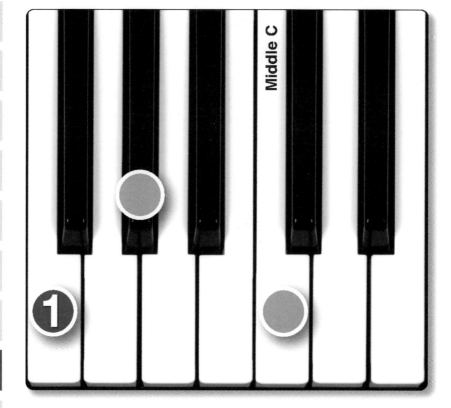

## Chord Spelling
1st (F), ♭3rd (A♭), 5th (C)
## Left Hand

**FREE ACCESS** on iPhone & Android
etc, using any free QR code app

Scan to **HEAR** this chord, or go directly
to flametreepublishing.com

# Fm
## Minor

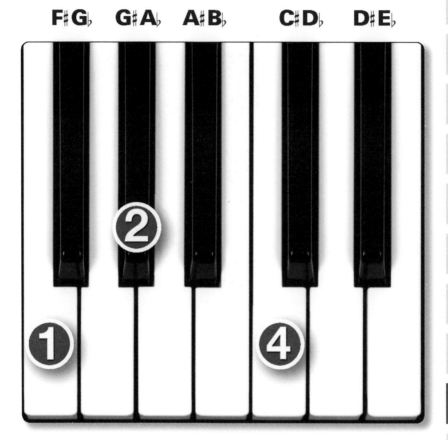

F#G♭  G#A♭  A#B♭      C#D♭   D#E♭

F  G  A  B  C  D  E

### Chord Spelling
1st (F), ♭3rd (A♭), 5th (C)
### Right Hand

START HERE

THE BASICS

A

A#/B♭

B

C

C#/D♭

D

D#/E♭

E

F

F#/G♭

G

G#/A♭

CHORDS IN CONTEXT

**FREE ACCESS** on iPhone & Android etc, using any free QR code app

Scan to **HEAR** this chord, or go directly to flametreepublishing.com

# Fsus4
## Suspended 4th

START
HERE

THE
BASICS

A

A#/B♭

B

C

C#/D♭

D

D#/E♭

E

**F**

F#/G♭

G

G#/A♭

CHORDS IN
CONTEXT

F#G♭   G#A♭   A#B♭        C#D♭   D#E♭

F    G    A    B    C    D    E

### Chord Spelling
1st (F), 4th (B♭), 5th (C)

**FREE ACCESS** on iPhone & Android
etc, using any free QR code app

Scan to **HEAR** this chord, or go directly
to flametreepublishing.com

# Fmaj7
## Major 7th

START HERE

THE BASICS

A

A#/Bb

B

C

C#/Db

D

D#/Eb

E

F

F#/Gb

G

G#/Ab

CHORDS IN CONTEXT

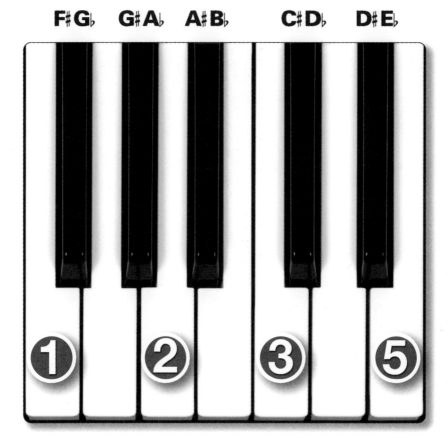

F#Gb   G#Ab   A#Bb      C#Db    D#Eb

① ② ③ ⑤

F   G   A   B   C   D   E

### Chord Spelling
1st (F), 3rd (A), 5th (C), 7th (E)

FREE ACCESS on iPhone & Android etc, using any free QR code app

Scan to HEAR this chord, or go directly to flametreepublishing.com

# F7
## Dominant 7th

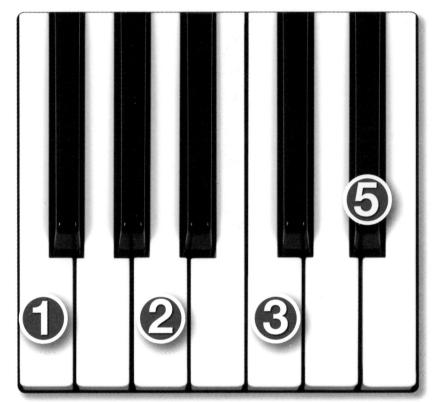

**F#G♭**  **G#A♭**  **A#B♭**    **C#D♭**  **D#E♭**

F    G    A    B    C    D    E

### Chord Spelling
1st (F), 3rd (A), 5th (C), ♭7th (E♭)

**FREE ACCESS** on iPhone & Android etc, using any free QR code app

Scan to **HEAR** this chord, or go directly to flametreepublishing.com

**START HERE**

**THE BASICS**

A

A#/B♭

B

C

C#/D♭

D

D#/E♭

E

F

F#/G♭

G

G#/A♭

**CHORDS IN CONTEXT**

# Fm7
## Minor 7th

START HERE

THE BASICS

A

A#/Bb

B

C

C#/Db

D

D#/Eb

E

F

F#/Gb

G

G#/Ab

CHORDS IN CONTEXT

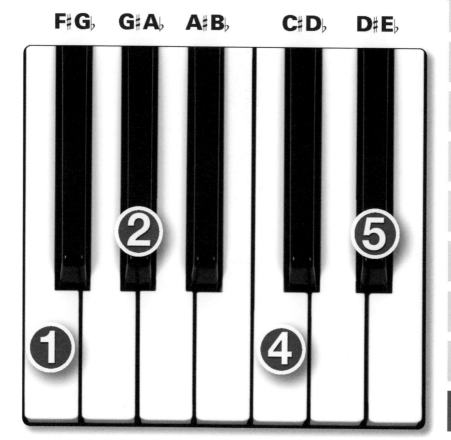

F#Gb   G#Ab   A#Bb   C#Db   D#Eb

F  G  A  B  C  D  E

## Chord Spelling

1st (F), b3rd (Ab), 5th (C), b7th (Eb)

**FREE ACCESS** on iPhone & Android etc, using any free QR code app

Scan to **HEAR** this chord, or go directly to flametreepublishing.com

# F♯/G♭
## Major

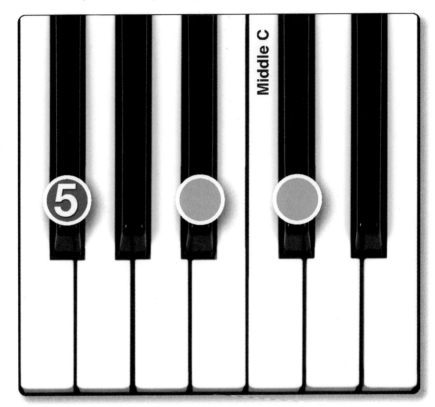

F♯G♭  G♯A♭  A♯B♭  C♯D♭  D♯E♭

Middle C

F   G   A   B   C   D   E

### Chord Spelling
1st (F♯), 3rd (A♯), 5th (C♯)

## Left Hand

**FREE ACCESS** on iPhone & Android etc, using any free QR code app

Scan to **HEAR** this chord, or go directly to flametreepublishing.com

Sidebar navigation:
START HERE
THE BASICS
A
A♯/B♭
B
C
C♯/D♭
D
D♯/E♭
E
F
F♯/G♭
G
G♯/A♭
CHORDS IN CONTEXT

# F♯/G♭
## Major

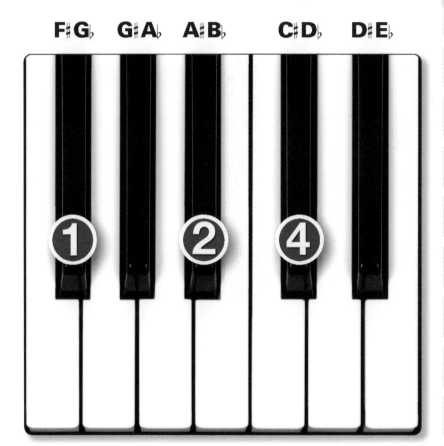

### Chord Spelling
1st (F♯), 3rd (A♯), 5th (C♯)
### Right Hand

**FREE ACCESS** on iPhone & Android etc, using any free QR code app

Scan to **HEAR** this chord, or go directly to flametreepublishing.com

START HERE

THE BASICS

A

A♯/B♭

B

C

C♯/D♭

D

D♯/E♭

E

F

F♯/G♭

G

G♯/A♭

CHORDS IN CONTEXT

# F♯/G♭m
## Minor

START
HERE

THE
BASICS

A

A♯/B♭

B

C

C♯/D♭

D

D♯/E♭

E

F

F♯/G♭

G

G♯/A♭

CHORDS IN
CONTEXT

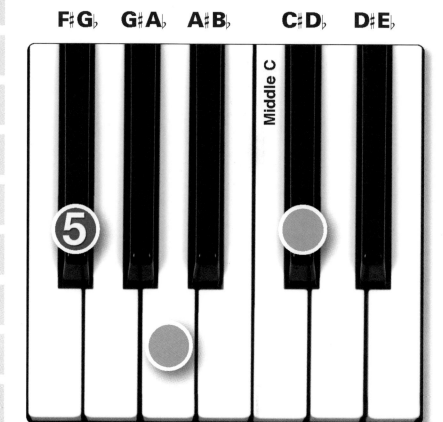

**F♯G♭   G♯A♭   A♯B♭       C♯D♭   D♯E♭**

Middle C

F   G   A   B   C   D   E

### Chord Spelling
1st (F♯), ♭3rd (A), 5th (C♯)

## Left Hand

**FREE ACCESS** on iPhone & Android
etc, using any free QR code app

Scan to **HEAR** this chord, or go directly
to flametreepublishing.com

# F#/G♭m
## Minor

F#G♭    G#A♭    A#B♭        C#D♭    D#E♭

F    G    A    B    C    D    E

## Chord Spelling
1st (F#), ♭3rd (A), 5th (C#)

## Right Hand

START HERE

THE BASICS

A

A#/B♭

B

C

C#/D♭

D

D#/E♭

E

F

F#/G♭

G

G#/A♭

CHORDS IN CONTEXT

**FREE ACCESS** on iPhone & Android etc, using any free QR code app

Scan to **HEAR** this chord, or go directly to flametreepublishing.com

115

# F#/G♭sus4
## Suspended 4th

START
HERE

THE
BASICS

A

A#/B♭

B

C

C#/D♭

D

D#/E♭

E

F

F#/G♭

G

G#/A♭

CHORDS IN
CONTEXT

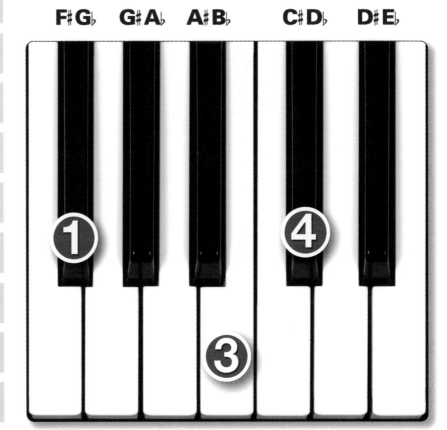

F#G♭  G#A♭  A#B♭    C#D♭   D#E♭

F G A B C D E

**Chord Spelling**
1st (F#), 4th (B), 5th (C#)

**FREE ACCESS** on iPhone & Android
etc, using any free QR code app

Scan to **HEAR** this chord, or go directly
to flametreepublishing.com

# F♯/G♭maj7
## Major 7th

START HERE

THE BASICS

A

A♯/B♭

B

C

C♯/D♭

D

D♯/E♭

E

F

F♯/G♭

G

G♯/A♭

CHORDS IN CONTEXT

G♯A♭  A♯B♭   C♯D♭  D♯E♭

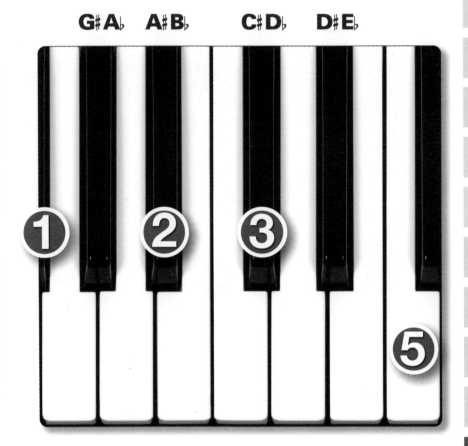

G  A  B  C  D  E  F

### Chord Spelling
1st (F♯), 3rd (A♯), 5th (C♯), 7th (F)

**FREE ACCESS** on iPhone & Android etc, using any free QR code app

Scan to **HEAR** this chord, or go directly to flametreepublishing.com

# F#/G♭7
## Dominant 7th

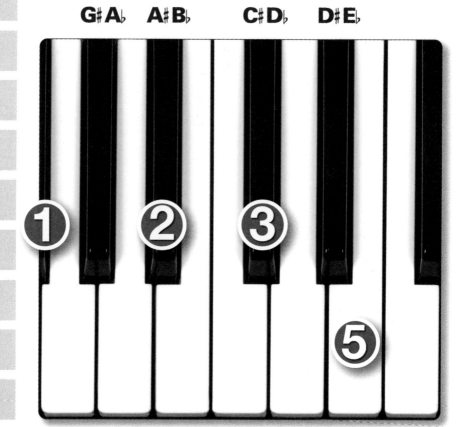

**Chord Spelling**
1st (F#), 3rd (A#), 5th (C#), ♭7th (E)

START
HERE

THE
BASICS

A

A#/B♭

B

C

C#/D♭

D

D#/E♭

E

F

F#/G♭

G

G#/A♭

CHORDS IN
CONTEXT

**FREE ACCESS** on iPhone & Android
etc, using any free QR code app

Scan to **HEAR** this chord, or go directly
to flametreepublishing.com

# F♯/G♭m7
## Minor 7th

START HERE

THE BASICS

A

A♯/B♭

B

C

C♯/D♭

D

D♯/E♭

E

F

F♯/G♭

G

G♯/A♭

CHORDS IN CONTEXT

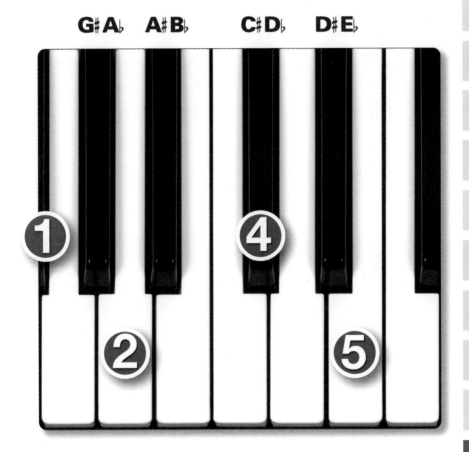

**Chord Spelling**

1st (F♯), ♭3rd (A), 5th (C♯), ♭7th (E)

**FREE ACCESS** on iPhone & Android etc, using any free QR code app

Scan to **HEAR** this chord, or go directly to flametreepublishing.com

# G
## Major

START HERE

THE BASICS

A

A#/Bb

B

C

C#/Db

D

D#/Eb

E

F

F#/Gb

G

G#/Ab

CHORDS IN CONTEXT

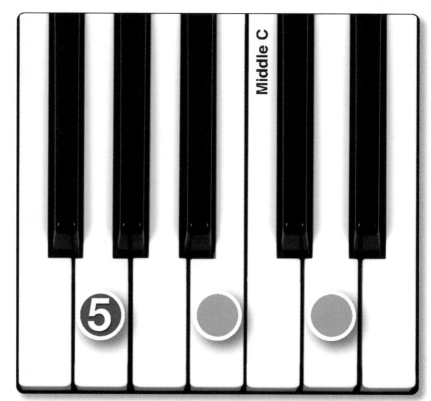

F#Gb    G#Ab    A#Bb         C#Db    D#Eb

Middle C

F    G    A    B    C    D    E

### Chord Spelling
1st (G), 3rd (B), 5th (D)
### Left Hand

**FREE ACCESS** on iPhone & Android etc, using any free QR code app

Scan to **HEAR** this chord, or go directly to flametreepublishing.com

# G
## Major

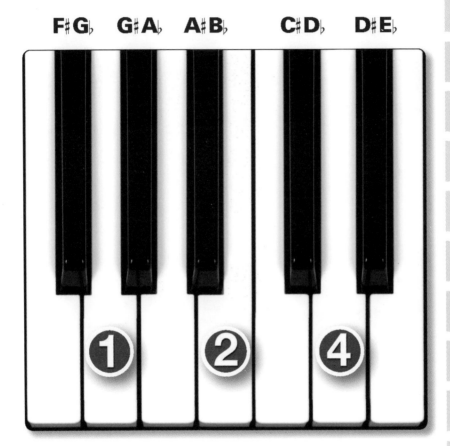

F#G♭  G#A♭  A#B♭   C#D♭   D#E♭

F  G  A  B  C  D  E

### Chord Spelling
1st (G), 3rd (B), 5th (D)

## Right Hand

START HERE

THE BASICS

A

A#/B♭

B

C

C#/D♭

D

D#/E♭

E

F

F#/G♭

G

G#/A♭

CHORDS IN CONTEXT

**FREE ACCESS** on iPhone & Android etc, using any free QR code app

Scan to **HEAR** this chord, or go directly to flametreepublishing.com

# Gm
## Minor

START
HERE

THE
BASICS

A

A#/Bb

B

C

C#/Db

D

D#/Eb

E

F

F#/Gb

G

G#/Ab

CHORDS IN
CONTEXT

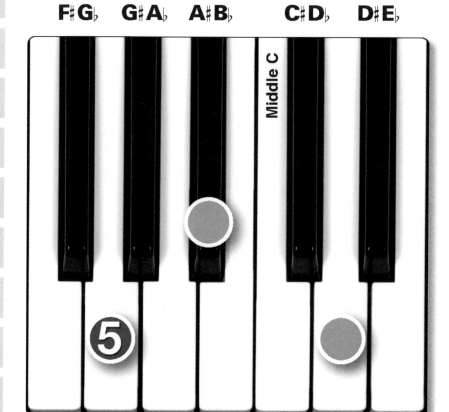

F#Gb    G#Ab    A#Bb        C#Db    D#Eb

Middle C

F    G    A    B    C    D    E

### Chord Spelling
1st (G), b3rd (Bb), 5th (D)
## Left Hand

**FREE ACCESS** on iPhone & Android
etc, using any free QR code app

Scan to **HEAR** this chord, or go directly
to flametreepublishing.com

# Gm
## Minor

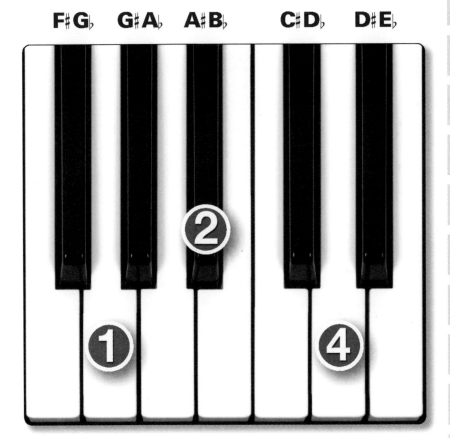

F#G♭  G#A♭  A#B♭     C#D♭   D#E♭

F  G  A  B  C  D  E

### Chord Spelling
1st (G), ♭3rd (B♭), 5th (D)
## Right Hand

START HERE

THE BASICS

A

A#/B♭

B

C

C#/D♭

D

D#/E♭

E

F

F#/G♭

G

G#/A♭

CHORDS IN CONTEXT

**FREE ACCESS** on iPhone & Android etc, using any free QR code app

Scan to **HEAR** this chord, or go directly to flametreepublishing.com

# Gsus4
## Suspended 4th

START
HERE

THE
BASICS

A

A#/Bb

B

C

C#/Db

D

D#/Eb

E

F

F#/Gb

G

G#/Ab

CHORDS IN
CONTEXT

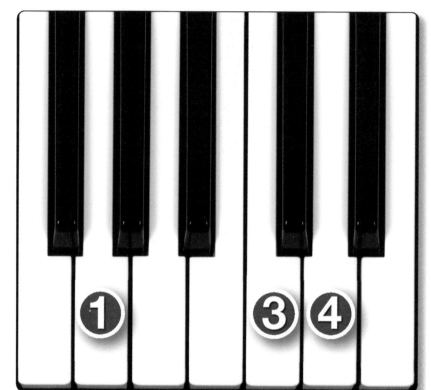

F#Gb   G#Ab   A#Bb     C#Db   D#Eb

**F  G  A  B  C  D  E**

### Chord Spelling
1st (G), 4th (C), 5th (D)

**FREE ACCESS** on iPhone & Android
etc, using any free QR code app

Scan to **HEAR** this chord, or go directly
to flametreepublishing.com

# Gmaj7
## Major 7th

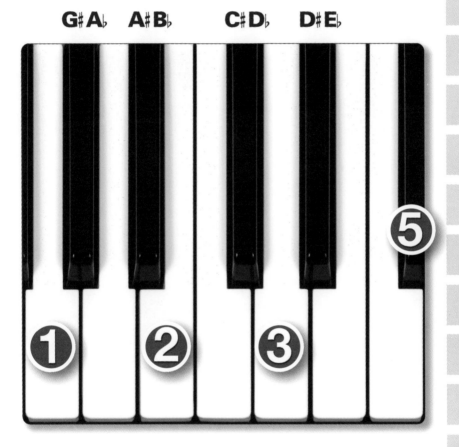

**Chord Spelling**
1st (G), 3rd (B), 5th (D), 7th (F♯)

START
HERE

THE
BASICS

A

A♯/B♭

B

C

C♯/D♭

D

D♯/E♭

E

F

F♯/G♭

G

G♯/A♭

CHORDS IN
CONTEXT

**FREE ACCESS** on iPhone & Android etc, using any free QR code app

Scan to **HEAR** this chord, or go directly to flametreepublishing.com

# G7
## Dominant 7th

START
HERE

THE
BASICS

A

A#/B♭

B

C

C#/D♭

D

D#/E♭

E

F

F#/G♭

G

G#/A♭

CHORDS IN
CONTEXT

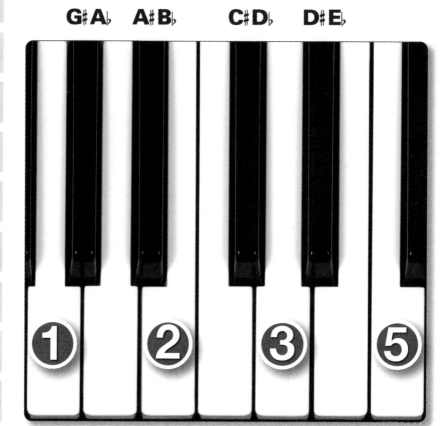

**G#A♭  A#B♭      C#D♭   D#E♭**

**G    A    B    C    D    E    F**

### Chord Spelling
1st (G), 3rd (B), 5th (D), ♭7th (F)

**FREE ACCESS** on iPhone & Android
etc, using any free QR code app

Scan to **HEAR** this chord, or go directly
to flametreepublishing.com

# Gm7
## Minor 7th

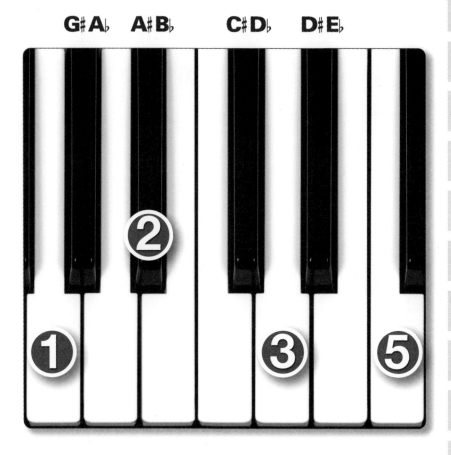

**G A B C D E F**

### Chord Spelling
1st (G), ♭3rd (B♭), 5th (D), ♭7th (F)

START HERE

THE BASICS

A

A♯/B♭

B

C

C♯/D♭

D

D♯/E♭

E

F

F♯/G♭

G

G♯/A♭

CHORDS IN CONTEXT

**FREE ACCESS** on iPhone & Android etc, using any free QR code app

Scan to **HEAR** this chord, or go directly to flametreepublishing.com

# G♯/A♭
## Major

START
HERE

THE
BASICS

A

A♯/B♭

B

C

C♯/D♭

D

D♯/E♭

E

F

F♯/G♭

G

G♯/A♭

CHORDS IN
CONTEXT

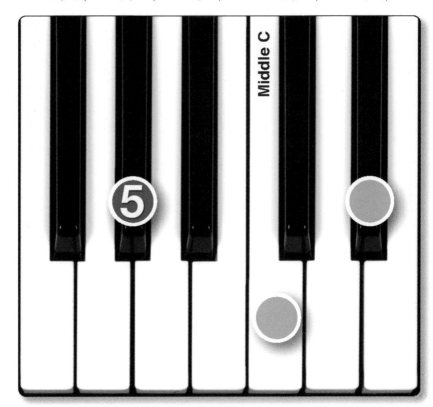

**F♯G♭  G♯A♭  A♯B♭    C♯D♭   D♯E♭**

Middle C

⑤

**F   G   A   B   C   D   E**

## Chord Spelling
1st (A♭), 3rd (C), 5th (E♭)

## Left Hand

**FREE ACCESS** on iPhone & Android
etc, using any free QR code app

Scan to **HEAR** this chord, or go directly
to flametreepublishing.com

# G♯/A♭
## Major

START HERE

THE BASICS

A

A♯/B♭

B

C

C♯/D♭

D

D♯/E♭

E

F

F♯/G♭

G

G♯/A♭

CHORDS IN CONTEXT

**F♯G♭**  **G♯A♭**  **A♯B♭**  **C♯D♭**  **D♯E♭**

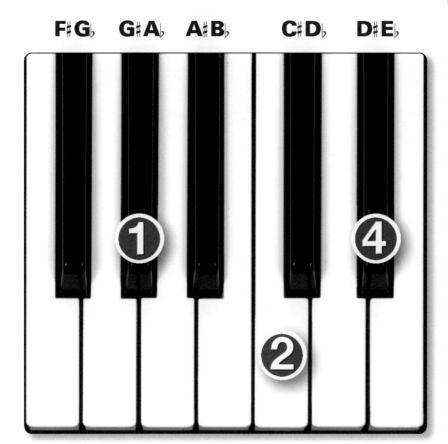

**F  G  A  B  C  D  E**

### Chord Spelling
1st (A♭), 3rd (C), 5th (E♭)

### Right Hand

**FREE ACCESS** on iPhone & Android etc, using any free QR code app

Scan to **HEAR** this chord, or go directly to flametreepublishing.com

129

# G♯/A♭m
## Minor

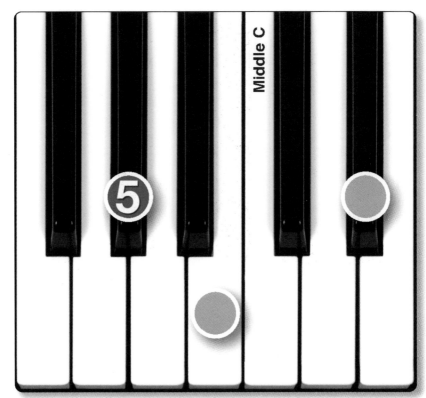

### Chord Spelling
1st (A♭), ♭3rd (C♭), 5th (E♭)

### Left Hand

**FREE ACCESS** on iPhone & Android
etc, using any free QR code app

Scan to **HEAR** this chord, or go directly
to flametreepublishing.com

# G#/A♭m
## Minor

START HERE

THE BASICS

A

A#/B♭

B

C

C#/D♭

D

D#/E♭

E

F

F#/G♭

G

G#/A♭

CHORDS IN CONTEXT

F#G♭   G#A♭   A#B♭      C#D♭   D#E♭

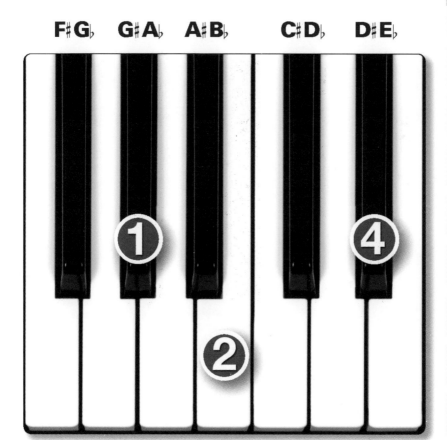

F    G    A    B    C    D    E

### Chord Spelling
1st (A♭), ♭3rd (C♭), 5th (E♭)
### Right Hand

**FREE ACCESS** on iPhone & Android etc, using any free QR code app

Scan to **HEAR** this chord, or go directly to flametreepublishing.com

131

# G♯/A♭sus4
## Suspended 4th

START
HERE

THE
BASICS

A

A♯/B♭

B

C

C♯/D♭

D

D♯/E♭

E

F

F♯/G♭

G

G♯/A♭

CHORDS IN
CONTEXT

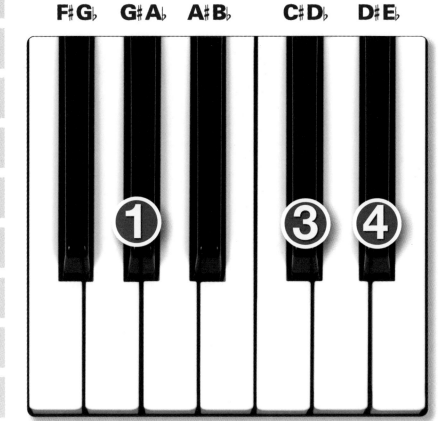

**F♯G♭  G♯A♭  A♯B♭    C♯D♭    D♯E♭**

F  G  A  B  C  D  E

### Chord Spelling
1st (A♭), 4th (D♭), 5th (E♭)

**FREE ACCESS** on iPhone & Android
etc, using any free QR code app

Scan to **HEAR** this chord, or go directly
to flametreepublishing.com

# G#/Abmaj7
## Major 7th

A#Bb    C#Db    D#Eb    F#Gb

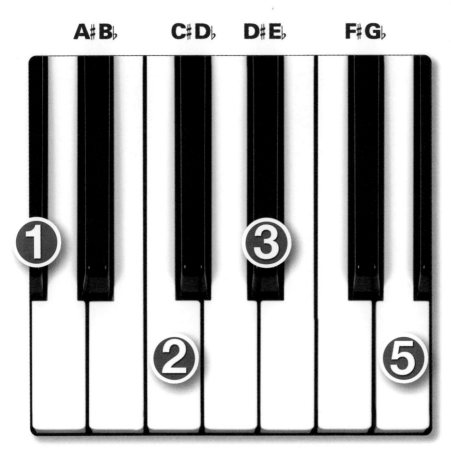

A    B    C    D    E    F    G

## Chord Spelling
1st (Ab), 3rd (C), 5th (Eb), 7th (G)

START
HERE

THE
BASICS

A

A#/Bb

B

C

C#/Db

D

D#/Eb

E

F

F#/Gb

G

G#/Ab

CHORDS IN
CONTEXT

**FREE ACCESS** on iPhone & Android etc,
using any free QR code app

Scan to **HEAR** this chord, or go directly
to flametreepublishing.com

# G♯/A♭7
## Dominant 7th

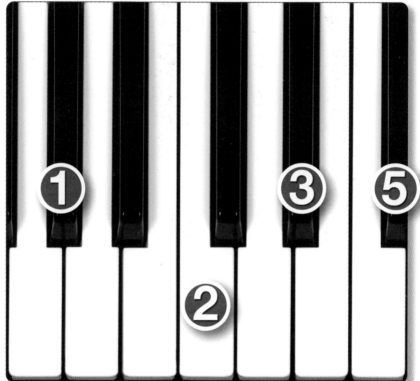

**Chord Spelling**

1st (A♭), 3rd (C), 5th (E♭), ♭7th (G♭)

START HERE

THE BASICS

A

A♯/B♭

B

C

C♯/D♭

D

D♯/E♭

E

F

F♯/G♭

G

G♯/A♭

CHORDS IN CONTEXT

**FREE ACCESS** on iPhone & Android etc, using any free QR code app

Scan to **HEAR** this chord, or go directly to flametreepublishing.com

# G♯/A♭m7
## Minor 7th

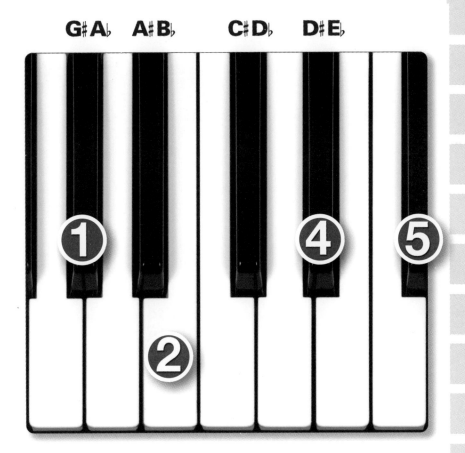

**G♯A♭**    **A♯B♭**    **C♯D♭**    **D♯E♭**

G    A    B    C    D    E    F

### Chord Spelling
1st (A♭), ♭3rd (C♭), 5th (E♭), ♭7th (G♭)

START HERE

THE BASICS

A

A♯/B♭

B

C

C♯/D♭

D

D♯/E♭

E

F

F♯/G♭

G

G♯/A♭

CHORDS IN CONTEXT

**FREE ACCESS** on iPhone & Android etc, using any free QR code app

Scan to **HEAR** this chord, or go directly to flametreepublishing.com

# Chords in Context

Once you're familiar with the common chords shown in the chord section, the next step is to learn how to properly use and combine them to create great music.

In this chapter you will find more advanced techniques, aimed to build on the basic skills and theory outlined in the first section of this book. As well as advice on putting chords together, you'll find examples of chord progressions to help get you started with popular chord combinations in any key. It's possible to use the main chords in loads of different ways too, so we've included tips on developing your own playing style and experimenting with different sounds using just a few chords. And, if you're hungry for more chord types, you can learn about augmented and diminished triads, sus2 chords, power chords, 6th chords, altered chords and extended chords (9ths, 11ths, 13ths etc) to really expand your chord vocabulary.

**This section will cover:**

- Techniques for smooth chord transitions
- Basic chord charts explained
- An example of a common chord progression in C
- Using the chord progression in other common keys
- Incorporating 7th chords
- Other variations on the common chord sequence
- Stylistic choices and ways to play the same chords
- Possible chord inversions, shown with C major
- An introduction to more advanced chords

**FREE ACCESS** on iPhone & Android etc, using any free QR code app

Scan to **HEAR** the C major chord, and access the full library of scales and chords on flametreemusic.com

START
HERE

THE
BASICS

A

A#/Bb

B

C

C#/Db

D

D#/Eb

E

F

F#/Gb

G

G#/Ab

CHORDS IN
CONTEXT

**FREE ACCESS** on iPhone & Android etc, using any free QR code app

Scan to **HEAR** the C major chord, and access the full library of scales and chords on flametreemusic.com

# Combining Chords

## Shared Notes

START
HERE

THE
BASICS

**Always look for links, or common notes, between consecutive chords, so you can minimize movement when changing chords. You may be able to keep some fingers on, or at least only move them slightly towards the next chord.**

Using **inversions** can create smoother transitions between chords. Inversions are covered on pages 156–57 but you can see them in action below in two examples of the C major triad moving to other chords.

In the first example, the second chord is **A minor**. This chord shares two of the same notes as C major (C and E), so using an inverted version of it means that only the G has to move to the A for the chord to change to A minor.

In the second example, the C chord moves to **G major**. These only have one note in common (G), but using an inversion of G major allows the bottom two notes of the C chord to only move down a step each to produce the G chord.

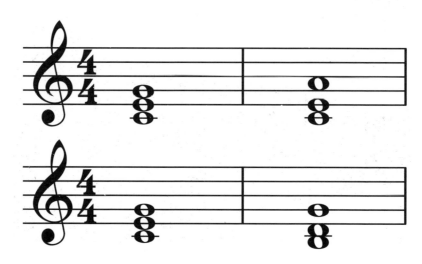

CHORDS IN
CONTEXT

**FREE ACCESS** on iPhone & Android
etc, using any free QR code app

Scan to **HEAR** the C major chord, and access the full library of scales and chords on flametreemusic.com

START
HERE

THE
BASICS

A

A#/B♭

B

C

C#/D♭

D

D#/E♭

E

F

F#/G♭

G

G#/A♭

CHORDS IN
CONTEXT

**FREE ACCESS** on iPhone & Android etc, using any free QR code app

Scan to **HEAR** the C major chord, and access the full library of scales and chords on flametreemusic.com

# Technique

**There are many ways to improve your playing, both to make it sound better and to make it easier on the hands. Here are some reminders of the most important points:**

- Keep your hand relaxed
- Fingers should be gently curved
- Your arm should feel like it is floating along

It's also possible to play the same notes differently to produce very different effects. For example, you can play individual notes smoothly running on from each other (**legato**), or much more detached (**staccato**), with each note stopping sharply before the next.

separated    legato    staccato

## Left Hand Technique

Usually, a melody is played by the right hand while the left hand accompanies with chord-based harmony. There are several different ways the left hand can use chords to accompany a melody. You can use:

- Single notes
- Simple chords
- Arpeggios and other broken chords
- Melodic lines that 'fit' in with the tune

**FREE ACCESS** on iPhone & Android etc, using any free QR code app

Scan to **HEAR** the C major chord, and access the full library of scales and chords on flametreemusic.com

START HERE · THE BASICS · A · A#/Bb · B · C · C#/Db · D · D#/Eb · E · F · F#/Gb · G · G#/Ab · CHORDS IN CONTEXT

On pages 155–57 there is more advice on the many different ways to play chords, but below you will find some examples to try with the left hand.

## Simple Chordal Accompaniment

## Bass Note Plus Chord

## Broken Chord

## Arpeggio

## Broken Chord (Wider Range and Rhythmic Patterning)

## Bass Note and Chord (with Rhythmic Variation)

**FREE ACCESS** on iPhone & Android etc, using any free QR code app

Scan to **HEAR** the C major chord, and access the full library of scales and chords on flametreemusic.com

START HERE

THE BASICS

A

A#/Bb

B

C

C#/Db

D

D#/Eb

E

F

F#/Gb

G

G#/Ab

CHORDS IN CONTEXT

START
HERE

THE
BASICS

A

A#/B♭

B

C

C#/D♭

D

D#/E♭

E

F

F#/G♭

G

G#/A♭

CHORDS IN
CONTEXT

# Chord Charts

**Chord charts are a handy way to communicate information to other players, and also good for your own reference if you come up with a good combination of chords that you'll want to return to later.**

Simple chord charts are the most common way of notating the chord structure of a song or chord progression. In their most basic form, chord charts usually include:

- Vertical lines to indicate the start of a new measure
- Chord symbols to show which chords should be played
- Slash symbols signifying repeat chords

For example:

$$|C \; / \; / \; /|G \; / \; / \; /|$$

This would mean the C major chord is played four times, followed by four G major chords.

If there is no **time signature** specified then it's usually safe to assume that the music is in 4/4 time. So for the above you could play the C major chord four times over 4 beats, followed by the G major chord four times over 4 beats.

When more than one chord appears in a single measure it can be assumed that the measure is to be **evenly** spread between the chords.

On the following pages common combinations of four chords are shown using chord charts.

**FREE ACCESS** on iPhone & Android etc, using any free QR code app

Scan to **HEAR** the C major chord, and access the full library of scales and chords on flametreemusic.com

START
HERE

THE
BASICS

A

A#/B♭

B

C

C#/D♭

D

D#/E♭

E

F

F#/G♭

G

G#/A♭

CHORDS IN
CONTEXT

**FREE ACCESS** on iPhone & Android etc, using any free QR code app

Scan to **HEAR** the C major chord, and access the full library of scales and chords on flametreemusic.com

START
HERE

THE
BASICS

A

A#/B♭

B

C

C#/D♭

D

D#/E♭

E

F

F#/G♭

G

G#/A♭

CHORDS IN
CONTEXT

# Common Chord Combinations

**After learning the basic chords, the next step towards playing great music is knowing which chords sound well together. Over the following pages we'll introduce a common chord progression to help get you started with putting chords together.**

An incredibly popular chord progression is the **I V vi IV** progression.

To work out which chords these refer to in C major, we can look again at the C major scale:

| C | D | E | F | G | A | B |
|---|---|---|---|---|---|---|
| I | ii | iii | IV | V | vi | vii° |

For a reminder of which types of chords are represented by these roman numerals, see pages 18–19.

The **I V vi IV** progression in C, therefore, would use the following chords:

| C | G | Am | F |
|---|---|----|---|
| I | V | vi | IV |
| C major | G major | A minor | F major |

This could be shown as a chord chart, in standard 4/4 time (four beats per bar):

**| C / / / | G / / / | Am / / / | F / / / |**

**FREE ACCESS** on iPhone & Android
etc, using any free QR code app

Scan to **HEAR** the C major chord, and access the full library of scales and chords on flametreemusic.com

## C major
**Chord Spelling**

1st (C), 3rd (E), 5th (G)

## G major
**Chord Spelling**

1st (G), 3rd (B), 5th (D)

## A minor
**Chord Spelling**

1st (A), ♭3rd (C), 5th (E)

## F major
**Chord Spelling**

1st (F), 3rd (A), 5th (C)

**FREE ACCESS** on iPhone & Android etc, using any free QR code app

Scan to **HEAR** the C major chord, and access the full library of scales and chords on flametreemusic.com

# In Other Keys

When chords and chord progressions are described in terms of roman numerals, they can be understood in terms of any key. The **I  V  vi  IV** progression shown in C on pages 144–45 can therefore be applied to other keys.

After C major, some of the other most common keys include D major, E major, G major and A major. Here, we'll show which chords are needed in each of these keys to produce **I  V  vi  IV**. The chord diagrams for these will follow on pages 148–151.

### D Major
In D major, the chords needed for the **I  V  vi  IV** progression are formed using the notes of the D major scale:

**D   E   F♯   G   A   B   C♯**

**I   ii   iii   IV   V   vi   vii°**

So the **I  V  vi  IV** combination of chords in D major could be played as:

**|D / / / | A / / / | Bm / / / | G / / / |**

### E Major
In E major, the chords needed for the **I  V  vi  IV** progression are formed using the notes of the E major scale:

**E   F♯   G♯   A   B   C♯   D♯**

**I   ii   iii   IV   V   vi   vii°**

**FREE ACCESS** on iPhone & Android etc, using any free QR code app

Scan to **HEAR** the C major chord, and access the full library of scales and chords on flametreemusic.com

So the **I  V  vi  IV** combination of chords in E major could be played as:

## |E / / / | B / / / | C#m / / / | A / / / |

**G Major**

In G major, the chords needed for the **I  V  vi  IV** progression are formed using the notes of the G major scale:

## G  A  B  C  D  E  F#

## I   ii   iii  IV   V   vi   vii°

So the **I  V  vi  IV** combination of chords in D major could be played as:

## |G / / / | D / / / | Em / / / | C / / / |

**A Major**

In A major, the chords needed for the **I  V  vi  IV** progression are formed using the notes of the A major scale:

## A  B  C#  D  E  F#  G#

## I   ii   iii  IV   V   vi   vii°

So the **I  V  vi  IV** combination of chords in D major could be played as:

## |A / / / | E / / / | F#m / / / | D / / / |

START
HERE

THE
BASICS

A

A#/B♭

B

C

C#/D♭

D

D#/E♭

E

F

F#/G♭

G

G#/A♭

CHORDS IN
CONTEXT

**FREE ACCESS** on iPhone & Android etc, using any free QR code app

Scan to **HEAR** the C major chord, and access the full library of scales and chords on flametreemusic.com

147

# I V vi IV in D major

START
HERE

THE
BASICS

A

A#/Bb

B

C

C#/Db

D

D#/Eb

E

F

F#/Gb

G

G#/Ab

CHORDS IN
CONTEXT

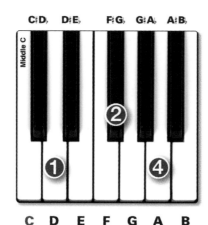

### D major
**Chord Spelling**
1st (D), 3rd (F#), 5th (A)

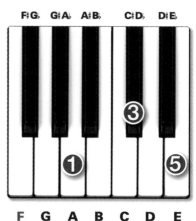

### A major
**Chord Spelling**
1st (A), 3rd (C#), 5th (E)

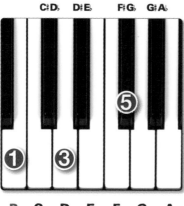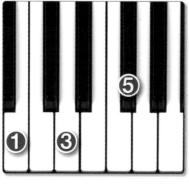

### B minor
**Chord Spelling**
1st (B), b3rd (D), 5th (F#)

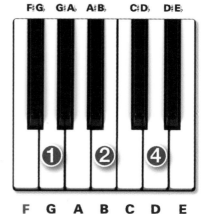

### G major
**Chord Spelling**
1st (G), 3rd (B), 5th (D)

**FREE ACCESS** on iPhone & Android
etc, using any free QR code app

Scan to **HEAR** the C major chord, and
access the full library of scales and
chords on flametreemusic.com

# I  V  vi  IV  in E major

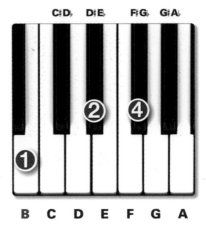

**C♯D♭  D♯E♭  F♯G♭  G♯A♭  A♯B♭**

Middle C

② ① ④

**C  D  E  F  G  A  B**

### E major
**Chord Spelling**
1st (E), 3rd (G♯), 5th (B)

**C♯D♭  D♯E♭  F♯G♭  G♯A♭**

② ④ ①

**B  C  D  E  F  G  A**

### B major
**Chord Spelling**
1st (B), 3rd (D♯), 5th (F♯)

**C♯D♭  D♯E♭  F♯G♭  G♯A♭  A♯B♭**

① ④ ②

Middle C

**C  D  E  F  G  A  B**

### C♯ minor
**Chord Spelling**
1st (C♯), ♭3rd (E), 5th (G♯)

**F♯G♭  G♯A♭  A♯B♭  C♯D♭  D♯E♭**

③ ⑤ ①

**F  G  A  B  C  D  E**

### A major
**Chord Spelling**
1st (A), 3rd (C♯), 5th (E)

**FREE ACCESS** on iPhone & Android etc, using any free QR code app

Scan to **HEAR** the C major chord, and access the full library of scales and chords on flametreemusic.com

START HERE

THE BASICS

A

A#/B♭

B

C

C#/D♭

D

D#/E♭

E

F

F#/G♭

G

G#/A♭

CHORDS IN CONTEXT

# I V vi IV in G major

START
HERE

THE
BASICS

A

A#/B♭

B

C

C#/D♭

D

D#/E♭

E

F

F#/G♭

G

G#/A♭

CHORDS IN
CONTEXT

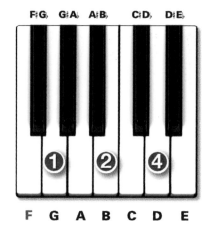

F♯G♭ G♯A♭ A♯B♭   C♯D♭ D♯E♭

F G A B C D E

### G major
**Chord Spelling**

1st (G), 3rd (B), 5th (D)

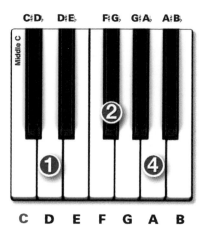

C♯D♭ D♯E♭   F♯G♭ G♯A♭ A♯B♭

C D E F G A B

### D major
**Chord Spelling**

1st (D), 3rd (F♯), 5th (A)

C♯D♭ D♯E♭   F♯G♭ G♯A♭ A♯B♭

C D E F G A B

### E minor
**Chord Spelling**

1st (E), ♭3rd (G), 5th (B)

C♯D♭ D♯E♭   F♯G♭ G♯A♭ A♯B♭

C D E F G A B

### C major
**Chord Spelling**

1st (C), 3rd (E), 5th (G)

**FREE ACCESS** on iPhone & Android
etc, using any free QR code app

Scan to **HEAR** the C major chord, and
access the full library of scales and
chords on flametreemusic.com

# I V vi IV in A major

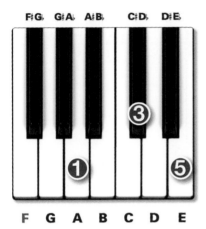

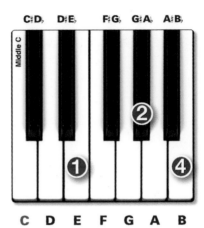

### A major
**Chord Spelling**

1st (A), 3rd (C♯), 5th (E)

### E major
**Chord Spelling**

1st (E), 3rd (G♯), 5th (B)

### F♯ minor
**Chord Spelling**

1st (F♯), ♭3rd (A), 5th (C♯)

### D major
**Chord Spelling**

1st (D), 3rd (F♯), 5th (A)

**FREE ACCESS** on iPhone & Android etc, using any free QR code app

Scan to **HEAR** the C major chord, and access the full library of scales and chords on flametreemusic.com

START HERE

THE BASICS

A

A♯/B♭

B

C

C♯/D♭

D

D♯/E♭

E

F

F♯/G♭

G

G♯/A♭

CHORDS IN CONTEXT

START
HERE

THE
BASICS

A

A#/B♭

B

C

C#/D♭

D

D#/E♭

E

F

F#/G♭

G

G#/A♭

CHORDS IN
CONTEXT

# Variations

It's possible to rearrange the chords in any progression to produce new progressions. For example, some different combinations of the **I V vi IV** could be:

- **I vi IV V** (in C: C, Am, F, G)
- **I V vi IV** (in C: C, G, Am, F)
- **vi IV I V** (in C: Am, F, C, G)
- **I IV vi V** (in C: C, F, Am, G)

These all use the same chords, but produce different musical effects when rearranged.

Other forms of variations when combining chords could be the substitution of other chords, or the embellishment of existing chords.

### Adding 7ths

One of the most commonly used chord embellishments is the addition of a **7th** note, which is why we've included three types of 7th chords in this book:

- **major seventh (maj7)**
- **dominant seventh (7)**
- **minor seventh (m7)**

The dominant seventh versions of the I, IV and V chords are especially useful. Dominant 7ths use the major triad, but with an added **flattened 7th**.

In C major, these three chords would be C7, F7 and G7. We can use their relevant scales to find the 'seventh' note in each case:

**FREE ACCESS** on iPhone & Android etc, using any free QR code app

Scan to **HEAR** the C major chord, and access the full library of scales and chords on flametreemusic.com

| C | D | E | F | G | A | B |
|---|---|---|---|---|---|---|
| F | G | A | B♭ | C | D | E |
| G | A | B | C | D | E | F♯ |
| I | ii | iii | IV | V | vi | vii° |

So adding a flattened 7th to each of the chords gives us:

$$
\begin{aligned}
I &= C &&(C, E, G)\\
I7 &= C7 &&(C, E, G, B♭)\\
IV &= F &&(F, A, C)\\
IV7 &= F7 &&(F, A, C, E♭)\\
V &= G &&(G, B, D)\\
V7 &= G7 &&(G, B, D, F)
\end{aligned}
$$

V7 chords are popular because all the notes in the chord can be found in the root key's major scale: here, all the notes in G7 are in the C major scale.

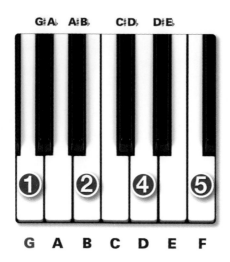

G7
**Chord Spelling**

1st (G), 3rd (B), 5th (D), ♭7th (F)

**FREE ACCESS** on iPhone & Android etc, using any free QR code app

Scan to **HEAR** the C major chord, and access the full library of scales and chords on flametreemusic.com

START HERE

THE BASICS

A

A♯/B♭

B

C

C♯/D♭

D

D♯/E♭

E

F

F♯/G♭

G

G♯/A♭

CHORDS IN CONTEXT

# Other Ways to Play Chords

**Usually when a chord chart is given you are expected to improvise over the chords shown, rather than simply play the chords one after the other. The following pages will show a few ways you can play with chords both in the harmony and melody of your music. A few things to bear in mind:**

- Look at the chords and make sure you know the notes for all of them.

- Think about the style and speed of the music.

- Do the chords change very quickly or will you be on each chord for a few beats?

- Look for common notes in consecutive chords.

- Can you see a bass line going through the chords?

- What sort of accompaniment are you going to play?

## Timing

Varying the timing in your chords and melody is one way to keep the sound interesting. For example, you can alter the number of notes per beat, or use combinations of short and long sounds, while still keeping a regular rhythm.

**FREE ACCESS** on iPhone & Android etc, using any free QR code app

Scan to **HEAR** the C major chord, and access the full library of scales and chords on flametreemusic.com

# Arpeggios and Broken Chords

When the notes of a chord are played individually, rather than at the same time, this is called an arpeggio. Using arpeggios can both reinforce the chord itself and lend an interest pattern to the melody or harmony.

It's helpful when first learning arpeggios to practise them in the set musical order they appear in the chord. Once you're familiar with the notes though you can mix up the order, repeat or omit notes, and vary the timing between notes to create combinations of short and long note lengths. This will produce a different type of broken chord, for example:

Below is another example of what you can do on top of a chordal accompaniment using notes from the chord:

FREE ACCESS on iPhone & Android etc, using any free QR code app

Scan to HEAR the C major chord, and access the full library of scales and chords on flametreemusic.com

START HERE

THE BASICS

A

A#/Bb

B

C

C#/Db

D

D#/Eb

E

F

F#/Gb

G

G#/Ab

CHORDS IN CONTEXT

# Chord Inversions

You may have seen in previous pages that chords are not always played in the strict order they are on the keyboard. Sometimes, when moving between chords it's easier to use inversions so that you don't have to move the whole hand to a new position for each chord. Inversions also help make the combined sound of chords more interesting. For example, here is the C major chord played with different parts of the chord as the lowest note:

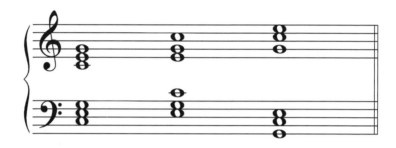

Inversions are normally notated as 'slash' chords:

## C/E is 'C major first inversion'

The lowest note of this triad is E, with G and C above it.

**FREE ACCESS** on iPhone & Android etc, using any free QR code app

Scan to **HEAR** the C major chord, and access the full library of scales and chords on flametreemusic.com

## C/G is 'C major second inversion'

The lowest note of this triad is G, with C and E above it.

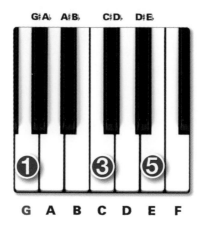

In a chord of 4 or more notes, it's possible for one of the extensions to be the lowest note. For example, 'C major 7 3rd inversion' uses the 7th as the bass:

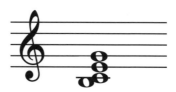

## Cmaj7/B is 'C major third inversion'

The lowest note of this chord is B, with C, E and G above it.

**FREE ACCESS** on iPhone & Android etc, using any free QR code app

Scan to **HEAR** the C major chord, and access the full library of scales and chords on flametreemusic.com

START HERE

THE BASICS

A

A#/Bb

B

C

C#/Db

D

D#/Eb

E

F

F#/Gb

G

G#/Ab

**CHORDS IN CONTEXT**

# Scales

**With a chord sequence, any notes you form a melody or solo from will sound best if they have mostly come from the key you're in.**

Scales are also a useful way of picturing the notes of a key in order. The C major scale has been shown already, but other useful ones are below.

## Major Scales in Other Keys

### G Major

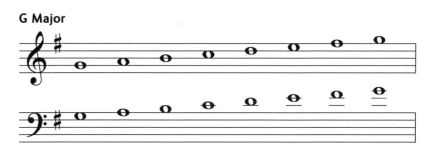

### D Major

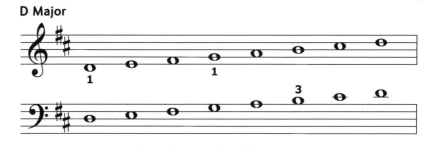

### A Major

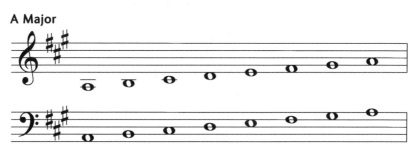

**FREE ACCESS** on iPhone & Android etc, using any free QR code app

Scan to **HEAR** the C major chord, and access the full library of scales and chords on flametreemusic.com

Sidebar navigation:
START HERE
THE BASICS
A
A#/Bb
B
C
C#/Db
D
D#/Eb
E
F
F#/Gb
G
G#/Ab
CHORDS IN CONTEXT

# Minor Keys

### C Harmonic Minor

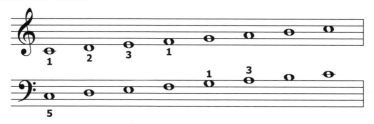

A simplified version of the minor scale that is especially useful for soloing is the Minor Pentatonic scale. This uses just 5 of the notes of the scale, so is more likely to sound 'in tune' with the main chords in the key. The notes in the C Minor Pentatonic scale are: C, E♭, F, G, B♭.

Be careful when using scales over chords not to let it sound too much like a scale. As with the chords, vary up your scales as much as possible.

# Chromatic Notes

To help colour a harmony you are improvising over you could add notes from outside the key you are in into the melody. Be careful not to introduce too many, so that it doesn't sound like you're moving key or lacking a tonal focus, but the odd extra note or two can add a sense of tension that can ultimately strengthen the notes of the chords when you return to them.

Here is the chromatic scale for reference. It uses all black and white keys:

**FREE ACCESS** on iPhone & Android etc, using any free QR code app

Scan to **HEAR** the C major chord, and access the full library of scales and chords on flametreemusic.com

| START HERE |
| THE BASICS |
| A |
| A♯/B♭ |
| B |
| C |
| C♯/D♭ |
| D |
| D♯/E♭ |
| E |
| F |
| F♯/G♭ |
| G |
| G♯/A♭ |
| CHORDS IN CONTEXT |

START
HERE

THE
BASICS

A

A#/Bb

B

C

C#/Db

D

D#/Eb

E

F

F#/Gb

G

G#/Ab

CHORDS IN
CONTEXT

Let's take a look at a simple chord progression:

**D | Bm | Em | A7**

In D Major, this progression could also be written as **I  vi  ii  V7**.

Begin by playing the root chords in both hands:

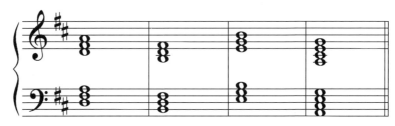

Now try playing them in inversion so you don't have to jump around:

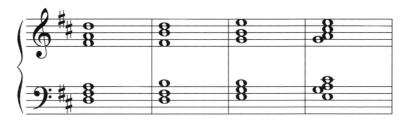

You could incorporate a 'walking bass'. Try this by seeing if there is a smooth route between the chords for the bass notes to run on without jumping more than a step away from each other:

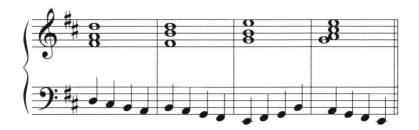

**FREE ACCESS** on iPhone & Android
etc, using any free QR code app

Scan to **HEAR** the C major chord, and access the full library of scales and chords on flametreemusic.com

You can also try a similar thing in the right hand, perhaps adding notes of different lengths to make it more interesting:

Then, combine the two – play the tune and the bass line, and include a few notes as chords to keep a strong sense of harmony:

You can apply a whole range of techniques to any combination of chords presented to you as a chord chart. Remember, start simple, then make them more adventurous when you have got the hang of it.

START
HERE

THE
BASICS

A

A#/Bb

B

C

C#/Db

D

D#/Eb

E

F

F#/Gb

G

G#/Ab

CHORDS IN
CONTEXT

**FREE ACCESS** on iPhone & Android etc, using any free QR code app

Scan to **HEAR** the C major chord, and access the full library of scales and chords on flametreemusic.com

# More Chords

This final section aims to introduce more chords into your repertoire. While that the chords already covered in this book are the ones you'll use the most, there are a few more types that it's useful to know about as they may crop up or come in handy during tricky chord combinations.

This section introduces the following more advanced chords:

- **Power Chords**
- **6th Chords**
- **Sus2 Chords**
- **Extended Chords: 9ths, 11ths and 13ths**
- **Altered Chords: Augmented and Diminished Triads, Diminished 7ths, and altered Dominant 7th chords (with flattened 5ths and flattened or sharpened 9ths)**

START
HERE

THE
BASICS

A

A#/B♭

B

C

C#/D♭

D

D#/E♭

E

F

F#/G♭

G

G#/A♭

CHORDS IN
CONTEXT

**FREE ACCESS** on iPhone & Android etc, using any free QR code app

Scan to **HEAR** the C major chord, and access the full library of scales and chords on flametreemusic.com

# Power Chords

Power chords unusually do not include a major or minor third; they consist only of the root note and the fifth. They are more common on the guitar, but can be useful on the piano too – for example, when you want to reinforce notes in a chord without committing to a major or minor sound. Often the root note will be duplicated at the octave to create a fuller sound. The below are all shown for the right hand, although it's useful to learn them in the left hand too.

**C5**
**Chord Spelling**
1st (C), 5th (G)

**D5**
**Chord Spelling**
1st (D), 5th (A)

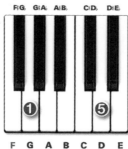

**E5**
**Chord Spelling**
1st (E), 5th (B)

**G5**
**Chord Spelling**
1st (G), 5th (D)

**A5**
**Chord Spelling**
1st (A), 5th (E)

**FREE ACCESS** on iPhone & Android etc, using any free QR code app

Scan to **HEAR** the C major chord, and access the full library of scales and chords on flametreemusic.com

START HERE

THE BASICS

A

A#/B♭

B

C

C#/D♭

D

D#/E♭

E

F

F#/G♭

G

G#/A♭

CHORDS IN CONTEXT

START
HERE

THE
BASICS

A

A#/Bb

B

C

C#/Db

D

D#/Eb

E

F

F#/Gb

G

G#/Ab

CHORDS IN
CONTEXT

# 6th Chords

This involves the sixth note of the major scale. For example, in C major:

## C D E F G A B C

A C6 chord (C major 6th) would consist of the regular C major triad notes: **C, E, G, plus the sixth note of the major scale: A.**

**Minor sixth chords** are formed in the same way, with the sixth note of the major scale added to the minor triad. So **Cm6** would be: **C, E♭, G, A.**
The C6 and Cm6 basic chord positions on the keyboard are shown below.

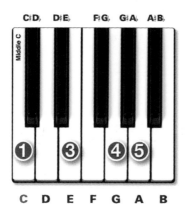

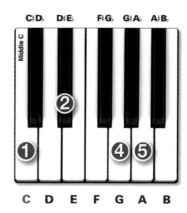

C6
**Chord Spelling**
1st (C), 3rd (E), 5th (G), 6th (A)

Cm6
**Chord Spelling**
1st (C), ♭3rd (E♭), 5th (G), 6th (A)

**FREE ACCESS** on iPhone & Android
etc, using any free QR code app

Scan to **HEAR** the C major chord, and
access the full library of scales and
chords on flametreemusic.com

# Sus chords

Sus chords are formed by **replacing** a note, rather than adding one. As well as the sus4 chords shown in this book, there are **sus2** chords, where it's the second note of the scale that replaces the chord's third. For example, **Csus2** is shown below, formed using the 1st (C), 2nd (D), and 5th (G) notes of the scale.

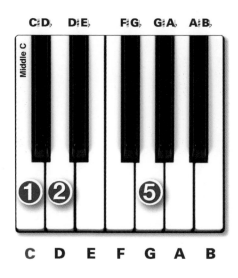

### Csus2
**Chord Spelling**
1st (C), 2nd (D), 5th (G)

# Extended Chords

Extended chords contain more notes. Just as 7th chords are built by adding an extra note to a basic triad, extended chords are built by adding one or more extra notes to a 7th chord. The most common types of extended chords are 9ths, 11ths and 13ths. Each can be played in either a major, minor or dominant form, and are shown on the following pages.

**START HERE**

**THE BASICS**

**A**

**A♯/B♭**

**B**

**C**

**C♯/D♭**

**D**

**D♯/E♭**

**E**

**F**

**F♯/G♭**

**G**

**G♯/A♭**

**CHORDS IN CONTEXT**

**FREE ACCESS** on iPhone & Android etc, using any free QR code app

Scan to **HEAR** the C major chord, and access the full library of scales and chords on flametreemusic.com

START
HERE

THE
BASICS

A

A#/Bb

B

C

C#/Db

D

D#/Eb

E

F

F#/Gb

G

G#/Ab

CHORDS IN
CONTEXT

## Major 9th

9th chords add the 9th note of the scale to the regular chord. Major 9th chords have a delicate sound that makes them highly suitable for use in ballads. They are extensions of major 7th chords, and are formed by adding the ninth note of the major scale (with the same starting note).

**Cmaj9** contains the notes of **Cmaj7**: C E G B;

plus the ninth note of the C major scale: **D**.

so Cmaj9 is: C E G B D

## Dominant 9th

Dominant 9th chords have a rich, bluesy sound. They are formed by adding the ninth note of the major scale to a dominant 7th chord.

**C9** contains the notes of **C7**: C E G Bb;

plus the ninth note of the C major scale: **D**.

So C9 is: C E G Bb D

**FREE ACCESS** on iPhone & Android
etc, using any free QR code app

Scan to **HEAR** the C major chord, and access the full library of scales and chords on flametreemusic.com

START
HERE

THE
BASICS

A

A#/Bb

B

C

C#/Db

D

D#/Eb

E

F

F#/Gb

G

G#/Ab

CHORDS IN
CONTEXT

## Minor 9th

Minor 9th chords have a suave, mellow sound and are often used in soul and funk music. They are extensions of minor seventh chords, formed by adding the ninth note of the major scale. As in the previous examples shown, the notes can be spread between the right and left hand.

**Cm9** contains the notes of **Cm7**: C E♭ G B♭;

plus the ninth note of the C major scale: **D**.

So **Cm9** is: **C E♭ G B♭ D**

## Cadd9

The ninth note can also be added to a simple triad, as this creates a certain warmth when added to a basic major chord.

**Cadd9** contains the notes of the basic **C major triad**: C E G;

plus the ninth note of the C major scale: **D**.

So **Cadd9** is: **C E G D**

 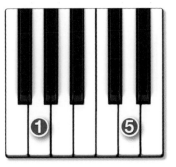

**FREE ACCESS** on iPhone & Android etc, using any free QR code app

Scan to **HEAR** the C major chord, and access the full library of scales and chords on flametreemusic.com

167

START
HERE

THE
BASICS

A

A#/Bb

B

C

C#/Db

D

D#/Eb

E

F

F#/Gb

G

G#/Ab

## Major 11th

11th chords extend chords even further, by adding the eleventh note on top of a ninth chord. Using the scale of C major as an example:

C D E F G A B C D E F

For all 11th chords, this eleventh note is added to either the major, minor or dominant chords, just as was done with the 9th chords (see pages 166–67).
**Cmaj11** contains the notes of **Cmaj9**: C E G B D;
plus the eleventh note of the C major scale: **F**.

So **Cmaj11** is: **C E G B D F**

CHORDS IN
CONTEXT

**FREE ACCESS** on iPhone & Android etc, using any free QR code app

Scan to **HEAR** the C major chord, and access the full library of scales and chords on flametreemusic.com

START
HERE

THE
BASICS

A

A#/B♭

B

C

C#/D♭

D

D#/E♭

E

F

F#/G♭

G

G#/A♭

CHORDS IN
CONTEXT

## Dominant 11th

Dominant 11th chords are formed by adding the eleventh note of the major scale to a dominant 7th or **dominant 9th chord**.

**C11** contains the notes of **C9**: C E G B♭ D;

plus the eleventh note of the C major scale: **F**.

So **C11** is: **C E G B♭ D F**

## Minor 11th

Minor 11th chords are formed by adding the eleventh note of the major scale to a minor 7th or **minor 9th chord**.

**Cm11** contains the notes of **Cm9**: C E♭ G B♭ D;

plus the eleventh note of the C major scale: **F**.

So **Cm11** is: **C E♭ G B♭ D F**

**FREE ACCESS** on iPhone & Android etc, using any free QR code app

Scan to **HEAR** the C major chord, and access the full library of scales and chords on flametreemusic.com

START
HERE

THE
BASICS

A

A#/Bb

B

C

C#/Db

D

D#/Eb

E

F

F#/Gb

G

G#/Ab

CHORDS IN
CONTEXT

## Major 13th

As with 9th and 11th chords, there are 3 main types of 13th chords too: major, dominant and minor versions. Each follows the same technique, using the core triad, and adding the 7th, 9th, 11th and now 13th note above.

For example, using the C major scale:

C  D  E  F  G  A  B  C  D  E  F  G  A

Again, the large amount of notes can be spread between right and left hands.

**Cmaj13** contains the notes of **Cmaj11**: C E G B D F;

plus the thirteenth note of the C major scale: **A**.

So **Cmaj13** is: **C E G B D F A**

**FREE ACCESS** on iPhone & Android
etc, using any free QR code app

Scan to **HEAR** the C major chord, and access the full library of scales and chords on flametreemusic.com

## Dominant 13th

Dominant 13th chords are formed by adding the thirteenth note of the major scale to a dominant chord.

**C13** contains the notes of **C11**: C E G B♭ D F;

plus the thirteenth note of C major scale: **A**.

So **Cm11** is: **C E G B♭ D F A**

## Minor 13th

Minor 13th chords are formed by adding the thirteenth note of the major scale to a minor chord.

**Cm13** contains the notes of **Cm11**: C E♭ G B♭ D F;

plus the thirteenth note of the C major scale: **A**.

So **Cm13** is: **C E♭ G B♭ D F A**

# Altered Chords

Altered chords provide an ideal method of creating a sense of tension and adding harmonic dissonance to a chord progression.

**Augmented triad:** **+**

**Diminished triad:** **°**

**Diminished 7th:** **°7**

**Dominant 7th♭5:** **7♭5**

**Dominant 7th♭9:** **7♭9**

**Dominant 7th♯9:** **7♯9**

**FREE ACCESS** on iPhone & Android etc, using any free QR code app

Scan to **HEAR** the C major chord, and access the full library of scales and chords on flametreemusic.com

# Augmented Triad

Augmented triads consist of a 5th that is raised a semitone, or half step, from its position in the key. So in C+, the 5th is raised a semitone from G to G♯.

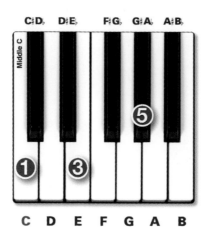

# Diminished Triad

Diminished triads consist of minor thirds stacked on top of each other. So the C° triad involves a minor 3rd (E♭) and a minor third on top (G♭).

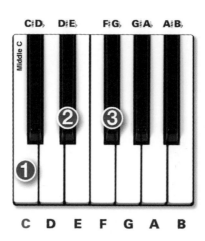

**FREE ACCESS** on iPhone & Android etc, using any free QR code app

Scan to **HEAR** the C major chord, and access the full library of scales and chords on flametreemusic.com

START HERE

THE BASICS

A

A♯/B♭

B

C

C♯/D♭

D

D♯/E♭

E

F

F♯/G♭

G

G♯/A♭

CHORDS IN CONTEXT

START
HERE

THE
BASICS

A

A#/Bb

B

C

C#/Db

D

D#/Eb

E

F

F#/Gb

G

G#/Ab

CHORDS IN
CONTEXT

# Resources

Here are a few companion titles that could come in useful if you intend to develop your skills playing and songwriting for the piano.

Also complementing this series is the audio library of chords and scales on **flametreemusic.com**, more details of which can be found on page 176.

## Piano Chords

Once you're familiar with the basic chords in this book, you can find a fuller range of more advanced chords in *Pick Up & Play Piano Chords*. With one diagram per page, this book is a quick reference tool for a wide range of useful chords in each key.

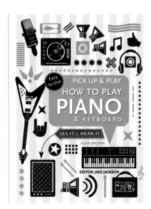

## How to Play Piano and Keyboard

With advice on notation, expression and technique, this book is designed for those just starting out with their piano-playing. Practical advice is accompanied by useful diagrams and charts, covering everything from rhythm and timing to notes and scales.

**FREE ACCESS** on iPhone & Android etc, using any free QR code app

Scan to **HEAR** the C major chord, and access the full library of scales and chords on flametreemusic.com

## Scales for Great Solos

A guide to the most common scales in all the keys, clearly laid out with one scale per page with links to **flametreemusic.com** so you can hear how each scale sounds. Also includes tips on soloing, and the best scales to use for different chords and music styles.

## How to Read Music: Essential Skills

The essentials for understanding music notation: pitch, clefs, rhythm, keys, scales and chords. Useful for both reading music and writing your own. Great for piano, keyboard and guitar, or for just brushing up on your music theory generally.

## Complete Beginners Chords for Guitar

We have a range of titles available for chords on the guitar too. If you're new to the guitar, our *Complete Beginners Chords for Guitar* covers the same basic chords and theory as our piano version. The book includes clear diagrams for the most useful guitar chords, plus extra tips on how to play and combine chords in a variety of ways.

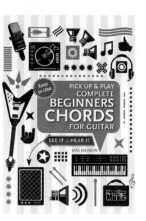

All available at your local independent bookshop, instrument store, online, or direct from **flametreepublishing.com**.

**FREE ACCESS** on iPhone & Android etc, using any free QR code app

Scan to **HEAR** the C major chord, and access the full library of scales and chords on flametreemusic.com

START HERE

THE BASICS

A

A#/B♭

B

C

C#/D♭

D

D#/E♭

E

F

F#/G♭

G

G#/A♭

CHORDS IN CONTEXT

# flametreemusic.com

**The Flame Tree Music website complements our range of print books and offers easy access to chords and scales online, and on the move, through tablets, smartphones, and desktop computers.**

1. The site offers access to chord diagrams and finger positions for both the guitar and the piano/keyboard, presenting a wide range of sound options to help develop good listening technique, and to assist you in identifying the chord and each note within it.

2. The site offers 12 **free** chords, those most commonly used in bands and songwriting.

3. A subscription is available if you'd like the full range of chords, **50** for **each key**.

4. Guitar chords are shown with **first** and **second positions on the fretboard**.

5. For the keyboard, you can **see** and **hear** each note in **left-** and **right-hand positions**.

6. Choose the key, then the chord name from the drop down menu. Note that the **red chords** are available **free**. Those in blue can be accessed with a subscription.

7. Once you've selected the chord, press **GO** and the details of the chord will be shown, with chord spellings, keyboard and guitar fingerings.

8. Sounds are provided in four easy-to-understand configurations.

9. flametreemusic.com also gives you access to **20 scales for each key**.